MW00528409

ALL IS WELL

Albert S. Rossi, PhD

ANCIENT FAITH PUBLISHING   CHESTERTON, INDIANA

All Is Well
Copyright ©2020 Albert S. Rossi

Published by:
    Ancient Faith Publishing
    A Division of Ancient Faith Ministries
    P.O. Box 748
    Chesterton, IN 46304

ISBN: 978-1-944967-79-6

Library of Congress Control Number: 2020940568

Printed in the United States of America

Contents

Foreword

ALL IS WELL because the tomb is empty. All is well because God is good. All is well because God has given us people like Dr. Al Rossi, who have had the courage to live, love, and share.

This is not a book for the fainthearted. Al shares his life in what he calls a really real way, without polish or hiding. This is a sort of spiritual autobiography, offered in such a way that the reader can assess his own life and learn how to make holy choices to grow and repent. It is remarkably accessible, expressing the wisdom of the ages in simple, modern terms. This little book needs to be read the way the finest of delicacies are tasted. Read slowly, deliberately, honestly, and reflectively. Smell the aromas, delight in the beauty, and taste with conscious anticipation. This book is worth its weight in gold.

Al Rossi is a deeply devoted practicing Orthodox Christian who happens to have studied Eastern and Western spirituality, modern psychology, and other social sciences. He has lived in monasteries, been successfully married, and broken bread with many of the most famous and learned modern theologians and spiritual guides. He has spent time in books with the greatest of the spiritual saints and has made himself comfortable in their company. He knows how to apply the tools of prayer, silence, listening, insight, and wise practices to allow healing and growth to those who attend his retreats, seminars, and classes, as well as to those who seek his counsel in therapy. Al is also a leader of Orthodox clergy and clinicians who seek to develop their ministries and practices through collaboration and group learning.

In this little book, Al uses his own life and struggles to show how accessible God is, and how God can and will help us as He has helped Al. He demonstrates the spiritual process to conquer sin, addiction, bad feelings, and evil thoughts. He doesn't sugarcoat anything. He speaks plainly yet insightfully, simply yet profoundly.

St. Nicodemus of the Holy Mountain speaks of man as a macrocosmos in a microcosmos. By this he means that each of us is internally more complex than the cosmos we live in. We know that mankind has just begun to understand bits and pieces of the universe and how they work. If we understand ourselves and each other as vastly complex, we can better approach ourselves and each other with appropriate awe, mercy, and gentleness. Please read this book with appropriate awe, mercy, and gentleness for both this heroic author and yourself.

Al Rossi is a charming man to be with. Although highly

educated in many disciplines, well-travelled, and connected to some of the Church's greatest leaders, Al is disarming and accessible to everyone he meets, a humble man with a winning combination of skills and tools. In this book he shares his story and invites you to consider your own life as he shares his experiences. This book can be life-changing and formative for the reader, if the reader dares!

Bishop John
Antiochian Bishop of Worcester and New England

Introduction

WHILE I WAS DRIVING east on Interstate 80 one early Monday morning, a novel idea suddenly crossed my mind. I was returning from an Ancient Faith Ministries conference for authors and podcasters, where I had given a talk to more than eighty participants. During the conference I also had the opportunity to speak privately with some of the participants, many of them authors who shared that they were leaving the conference with renewed resolve to write more intentionally. The weekend over, I was happily driving home. The sun shone brightly; there was not a cloud in the sky. The drive was pleasant, and I was trying to be aware of God's presence. My consciousness flowed seamlessly.

The novel idea that suddenly crossed my mind was that I would never write another book—emphasis on the word *never*. I was done with that part of my life. Others could write books. I would do other things, like lead retreats, counsel, volunteer on committees, participate in conference calls, and teach at St. Vladimir's Seminary. But three weeks later, I was still doing these "other things," and I had thousands of words in draft form to begin another book—this book. Surprise.

We never know when surprises might happen. The Morning Prayer of Metropolitan Philaret says, "In unforeseen events let me not forget that all are sent by You." Most events are unforeseen. I don't know who might phone today, and I don't know how the rest of my life will unfold. The secret is to try to really trust that all of the surprises—what I call "suddenly" events—are sent by Christ.

About This Book

THOUGH I HAD MADE a decision about my priorities moving forward, my wife, Galina, in heaven had other ideas—she wanted to co-author another book with me. As I try to go through the semipermeable membrane of the Kingdom and listen to her, this kind of awareness can make for an exciting adventure. I don't know what God will send next, but I know that whatever it is, the next "suddenly" will be sent by God out of His tender love for me. And, for me, it will usually be sent through my wife.

As I began writing this little book, it seemed like doing a thousand-piece jigsaw puzzle of Monet's *Water Lilies*. Each piece looked the same as all the others, and the pile of pieces looked nothing like the picture on the box. As with the imagined puzzle, the book seemed doable but daunting.

In my early work on this book I went back and reread my two previous books: *Can I Make a Difference: Christian Family Life Today*, published by Paulist Press in 1990; and *Becoming a Healing Presence*, published by Ancient Faith Publishing in 2015. A few unexpected discoveries jumped out at me. First, I noticed that Father Thomas Hopko wrote an extended foreword to the first book, and he wrote an extended foreword to the second book. The twenty five-year span between the two books seemed to bookend his partnership with me as well as our friendship. He has been, and from heaven continues to be, a rock throughout the course of my career.

Another discovery I made when looking back at my first two books was that the second is much more personal than the first. The first book seems all right but rather bland—I would not recommend it. *Can I Make a Difference: Christian Family Life Today*. Intriguing title, but short on substance. My hope has been to make this third book more engaging than the two previous, with more personal narrative.

When I pause to think about the past, I realize that Father Hopko, my wife, and I have been working together for decades. That is more than I can comprehend. I also realize that I am the weak dancing partner in the troika. But the troika has been and is. Lord, have mercy.

It is also clear that "Unless the Lord builds the house, / Those who build it labor in vain" (Ps 126:1). So, too, unless the Lord writes and reads the book, those who write and read likewise do so in vain. Lastly, unless the Lord lives the life, those who live it live in vain. Let us hope and pray together that we do our best to remain in the Lord's presence and allow the Lord to move through us.

My hope is not to make this book a display, but a path to healing, in accordance with the words of St. Athanasius of Alexandria: "The Lord did not come to make a display. He came to heal and to teach suffering people."

I want to thank my professional editor, Julia Wickes, a long-time friend and colleague. Julia finely edited this book with precision and sharpness. Dr. Peter Bouteneff added to Julia's editing by fine-tuning the draft with exquisite comments. Katherine Hyde at Ancient Faith Publishing did an elegant final edit.

I have done my best not to repeat much, if anything, from my previous book, *Becoming a Healing Presence*. I have also tried to write conversationally. Therefore, I have tried to write patiently and slowly. I'll ask you to try to read this little book patiently and slowly.

CHAPTER I

Now, All Is Well

Father Hopko would often say, "All is well." I think I know what he meant by that, and I will revisit this later. Like Father Hopko, I too find myself saying "all is well" on a regular basis. Throughout this little book, I will expound on what this statement means to me. Most broadly, to say that all is well is to say that all in my life is sufficient. And that is saying a lot.

Father Hopko often quoted Julian of Norwich, who said, "All shall be well and all manner of thing shall be well." He would use a passage from Romans to strengthen his case that all is well, a verse we are all familiar with: "And we know that all things work together for good to those who love God, to those who are the called according to *His* purpose" (Rom. 8:28). This is the truth. It's also interesting for us to read the paragraph that goes before it:

> *Likewise the Spirit also helps in our weaknesses. For we do not know what we should pray for as we ought, but the Spirit*

Himself makes intercession for us with groanings which cannot be uttered. Now He who searches the hearts knows what the mind of the Spirit is, because He makes intercession for the saints according to the will of God. (Rom. 8:26, 27)

Father Hopko would also go on to quote one of his very favorite saints, St. Thérèse of Lisieux. She says, "Whatever be the character of life or its unexpected events—to the heart that loves, *all is well.*"

More Than Meets the Eye

IN THE EARLY STAGES OF WRITING, I described the idea of this little book to a colleague. He responded, "My, but that is a difficult topic." Well, yes, it is a difficult topic, and a delicate one. When I look at the front of the daily newspaper, it does not appear that all is well. When I try to discern the national and international scene, it does not appear that all is well. More importantly, when I look at the insides of my hard heart, it certainly does not seem that all is well.

I am a clinical psychologist. I deal with many people who have been victimized all over the place, and I deal with people who do, or did, some really awful victimizing. We don't deny evil where evil exists. Ugliness and corruption exist unabated. We live on a cracked and crazy planet. In the exploration of what it means to say that all is well, these hard realities are a good place to start. Without a doubt, this is a paradox. But many wise Orthodox teachers have observed that Orthodoxy is paradoxy.

We need to look at reality squarely and call good "good" and evil "evil." We need to see, not deny, the darkness and evil in our outer and inner worlds. I want to face this up front because it lies at the heart of the matter. But—and this is the tricky part—we also need to see *through* reality to the other side. We need to see the larger picture, the *other reality* that is also going on. If you don't mind, I'll say that we need to see reality from God's point of view. Now, obviously that is a difficult task, but not beyond our capability. Such a view is impossible, but possible by God's grace. The Angel Gabriel said to Mary, the Theotokos, "For with God nothing will be impossible" (Luke 1:37).

As St. John Chrysostom reminds us, "Happiness can only be achieved by looking inward and learning to enjoy whatever life has, and this requires transforming greed into gratitude." St. John Chrysostom, as often quoted by Father Hopko, is helping us look beyond what the eye sees and to look inward. What I am saying is that there is more to reality than meets the eye. As the Little Prince says in the book by the same name, "It is only with the heart that one sees rightly." We need to see reality from the *light* side of ourselves, the side of Christ within us.

When I give parish retreats, I often begin by showing a large colored photo on a screen, an image that shows two faces of the same girl side by side. On one side the girl is holding a lit candle, and her face is aglow with radiance. On the other side the same girl is holding the candle blown out. Her face is glum and forlorn. She blew out the candle and is now in darkness. The point is clear—as children of Adam and Eve, each of us has two basic selves inside, a light self and a dark self. The light side of us is the Light of Christ that we can accept or blow out, at least from our point of view. In truth, Christ never leaves us, but sets us free to leave Him if we choose.

I love our culture and love our world. I'm not unworldly except in the sense of the Gospel command that we are to be in the world, but not of it. We are to be fully invested in our family, neighborhood, national and international politics, and the planet, but with the mind of Christ—a mind that is alert, joy-filled, and loving. We are not to be obsessed with the anxiety that's also inside all of us as children of Adam and Eve. The world consists in ugliness, and the world consists in beauty. Without denying the ugliness, we are to keep our mind on the beauty, as best we can.

Growing Gradually

WE GROW FROM STAGE TO STAGE, usually unevenly and without assessing our growth. But we know that we have "grace upon grace," as St. John says (John 1:16, RSV). Our spiritual "growth spurts," so to speak, often happen as a result of failure and suffering. As Yoda says, "Failure, a great teacher is." We learn different lessons in a hospital bed than we learn in church school.

I learned a stinging yet profitable lesson when I was a senior in college. I was a lost soul who compensated by putting on an attractive exterior. I was president of the student council and a commissioned second lieutenant in the Army. I drove a little red convertible and had a fiancée who was everything a young man could want, including Queen of the Military Ball. She loved me dearly. Yet, deep inside, I knew that something was askew. Something inside was radically wrong, and I didn't know what.

One Sunday afternoon my fiancée and I were parked, talking about whatever. She turned to me and said, in a nonjudgmental, matter-of-fact voice, "Al, can I say something to you?"

I said, "Sure, honey."

She then said, "You talk a lot, but you don't say much."

I wasn't hurt, and I didn't respond. It was if she had said, "It looks like it might rain." I knew she was right. She knew she was right. I really couldn't say anything in response.

At the time I was numb to the reality of her words, except for the fact that I knew they were true, and important. Now I look back upon that sentence with embarrassment and bewilderment. I now know that at that moment I made a deep, unconscious resolution to reverse this equation. In a sense, I said to myself, "From now on I am going to speak less and say more." I couldn't articulate it then, but I knew I wanted something better for my life, something lofty, something transcendent, something noble. I wanted to have something to fight for, something for which to expend myself.

What she said was valid and struck a deep chord within me. I now know that her remark was a turning point in my life. I think her comment was a large factor in my doing what I then felt compelled to do—namely, entering a monastery after college and staying for eleven years. How that came about is another narrative for another time—perhaps, if God so chooses, a narrative for another book.

At the time my fiancée made that pronouncement, I was generally unaware and unrepentant (though I did have a vague awareness that all was not well with my attitude). Now a man in my eighties, I am comfortable enough with how much I talk and how much I don't talk. I am far from perfect, but not absurd, as I was as a college senior. Across the decades, by Christ's grace, we can grow and change.

Becoming Less Judgmental

ONE IMPLICATION OF "all is well" is that we don't have to judge others. Recently I passed an Asian Christian Church that had a small signboard in front. The sign read, "Don't judge others because they sin differently than we do." The sign sends the clear signal that we are all sinners and walk a similar path on this planet.

We don't become less judgmental by a quick resolution to stop judging. Consciously or unconsciously, we all judge others. We become less judgmental by catching ourselves judging others, then surrendering the judgment to the Lord. In that sense, judging others can be an opportunity to pray, to surrender, and to be less judgmental. God can do for us what we cannot do for ourselves.

Is My Life Sufficient?

WELL, YES AND NO. Sometimes my life seems sufficient, sometimes not. Sometimes I believe in my heart that my life is sufficient, sometimes not. We ask the Lord for growth in our perception of reality.

Our life, in a sense, is what we make of it. I would say that I am not lonely, simply because I have enough social interaction at St. Vladimir's Seminary. When I arrive at my little apartment in the evening I want time to decompress, alone. Some Saturday afternoons I do domestic chores: laundry, dishes, and vacuuming. I might say to the Lord, "Don't you want me to go to the Far East and convert infidels instead of pushing this broom?" Or "Lord, don't you want me to write a new article?" I don't get an audible response from the Lord, but I know that He wants me to be humble enough to realize that He, in His wisdom from all eternity, wants me to do laundry and not work on another article, at least until the domestic chores are completed.

We have the Bible to guide our best moments: "And my God shall supply all your need according to His riches in glory by

Christ Jesus" (Phil. 4:19). Yes, every need will be satisfied and supplied. Yes, all is well.

However, within us is a craving for more than we have. Sometimes this leads to an addiction of one sort or another. The essence of addiction is the word "more." The addicted overeater has an insatiable hunger for *more* food. A married man whose wife is attractive and sexually responsive can become addicted to internet pornography for *more* sexual stimulation. We can all be tempted to crave *more* of something—time, talent, wealth, health, friendship, different spiritual virtues, or whatever.

I am a recovering alcoholic who, by God's grace, has a bronze chip for twenty-six years of sobriety. But I know that I have an addictive personality. I have also been addicted to caffeine, nicotine, and sugar. When I was a young adult visiting my mother, I was unaware that I was drinking diet soda nonstop. My mother noticed my behavior and said simply, "Al, you could become addicted to carrots." She was right, because carrots have sufficient sugar to set off a craving in me. I also have a serious inclination—a craving—to believe that all is not well with me. Perhaps that is why I am writing this book, to help me embrace more fully the truth that all *is* well.

For me to say all is well can be a supreme challenge of faith, because "God is our refuge and power; / A help in afflictions that severely befall us" (Ps 45:2). It is God, not I, who makes all to be well. It is also true that our minds will fade in and out of confidence that all is well. That's OK. All God expects is that we do the best we can with what we have.

Introverts and Extroverts

BEFORE MOVING ON, I would like to touch on the subject of introversion and extroversion. I have found that insight into this distinction between two types of people is often at the foundation of arriving at the conclusion that all is well.

We can ask ourselves, "Am I an introvert or an extrovert?" I don't know anyone who is a hundred percent either introvert or extrovert. We're each a mixture of both. So this is really a question of proportion: Am I *more* of an introvert or an extrovert?

Without giving a technical definition, I'll simply say that introverts are those human beings who replenish their energy by being alone. I'll also say clearly that I'm more of an introvert. I live alone, and I love it. Many of my days are filled with people time at St. Vladimir's Seminary, counseling, having meals with the students, and talking to people. But when I come home in the evenings, I cherish my alone time because it fills my gas tank. I thrive on the high octane of solitude, when given the opportunity.

Extroverts, by contrast, renew their energy by talking to other people. My daughter Beth, sweetheart that she is, when she was a teenager seemed to be an extrovert, though she has mellowed greatly with the birth of her three children. When she was sixteen years old, I used to kid her and say, "Sweetheart, you walk around with a telephone duct-taped to your ear." Any time she had a problem or confusion in her head, she would talk to somebody; she would talk to me, she would talk to her mother when her mother was alive, she would talk to friends. In the conversation she would come up with answers, insight, and energy. Extroverts gain clarity of thought by speaking what is in their heads. New solutions then appear.

So that's the basic difference I will put out there for us. I will also say, just by way of implication from that construct, that introverts will find it more difficult to engage in social outreach, social interactions, and hospitality. They do it, of course, and can do it well. I'm an introvert, and I'm with people all day long. My daughter says to me that I talk a lot—I don't know about that, but my point is that it takes an extra oomph to do it. Extroverts, by implication, will find more difficulty, in general, meditating and making time for personal prayer, time to be alone with the Lord. Obviously, extroverts can do it very well, but it takes that extra oomph to do it.

Another important implication is that in close friendships or marriage, there's a tendency to project our own interior landscape onto other people. So if I'm an introvert, I tend to think that other people would have a little better life if they became more like me. If I happen to be an extrovert, I tend to think that others would have a little better life if they became more extroverted. Granted, that's a fatal notion, but we are children of Adam and Eve, and we behave that way. I can look back on my own marriage, and I can understand how my wife and I worked this out.

If I happen to be an introvert and my wife is an extrovert, then whenever we have some conflict between us, first thing she does might be to go to the telephone and talk out her issue. I might think to myself, and even say to her, "Why don't you just spend a little time alone getting some energy and reflecting on what's happening?" That, of course, is contraindicated. Conversely, if my wife is an introvert and I am an extrovert and we have conflict, I might tend to speak with a friend about the conflict and suggest that she do the same. But it is not helpful for one person to express an opinion about how the other should act. She might want to go into her room, close the door, and resolve her confusion. What we need is to learn to respect each other's space.

Carl Jung, the famous psychoanalyst who first elaborated the ideas of introversion and extroversion as we know them today, said that every human being is born with some slight imbalance one way or the other, and the task in life is to become balanced. Introverts can become more extroverted, and extroverts can become more introverted. That is, we are to find balance, equanimity, within our personality.

I can recall once encountering a book with a title that was something along the lines of, *Was Jesus an Introvert?* The book was entirely devoted to that question, and as I recall, the conclusion was that Jesus was an introvert, and we should all be more like Him—introverts. In my judgmentalism, I think an introvert probably wrote the book. Anyway, I don't particularly agree with that conclusion. I don't think that Jesus was either introvert or extrovert in these terms. I would say He was so fully human, so balanced, it wouldn't be fair to say that He was one or the other. Jesus is the model for us of choosing private time, often going alone to pray and be with His Father, but He was also certainly often in the midst of multitudes and meeting with His disciples. He is our model of both sides, of balance.

Whether I am an introvert or extrovert, I can be sure that I will have sufficient stamina and resources to do what the Lord has put me on the planet to do. St. Gregory of Nyssa said, "Who gives you the day will give you also the things necessary for the day."

CHAPTER 2

Ambiguity Revisited

PERHAPS THE MOST INTRIGUING CHAPTER from my book *Becoming a Healing Presence,* at least to those who choose to engage me in conversation about the book, is chapter 9, "Embracing Ambiguity." Many have asked for an expansion of the ideas in that chapter. So, here goes.

The handy little formula that I provided is: (a) I know that I don't know; (b) I know that Christ knows; (c) I try to trust Him. Oh, so simple and so hard to comprehend and live.

The hard part seems to be the awareness that I really don't know. But that's the hard truth. Speaking for myself and so many others, there is a control freak residing inside me, wanting to rear its ugly head at a moment's notice. Somehow, I believe that forewarned is forearmed in every eventuality. Yes, there is a benefit to being prepared, but that doesn't mitigate the deeper truth that I really don't know whether I will have a next God-given breath. The control freak continues to obsess over the "what ifs." As Mark Twain said, "I am an old man now and have had a great many problems. Most of them never happened."

Part of us wants to have everything spelled out clearly, to have all understood plainly, to get closure on questions that must be left open.

We can slip into delusion about how strong we are at any given moment. St. Anthony the Great said, "A time is coming when men will go mad, and when they see someone who is not mad, they will attack him, saying, 'You are mad; you are not like us.'" Not only is that true for others speaking about us, but it can be true about the way we speak to ourselves.

Unexpected News

ANOTHER HARD PART is that "suddenly" can happen at any moment.

One ordinary-enough afternoon, I was working at my computer in my little apartment. The phone rang. By the way, when the phone rings most people's stress level goes way up, simply because the message may be that we just won the lottery or that our credit card was compromised. Anyway, my phone rang.

My daughter, Beth, was on the other end of the line. She doesn't usually call in the middle of an afternoon. After a brief intro she said, "Dad, Greg [her husband] and I would like your opinion about a personal matter." I braced myself. She went on, "Six months ago I wanted a third child and Greg didn't. Now, he wants a third child and I don't. We both want to know what you think."

The implication was that my opinion would be part of the equation to settle the matter. I held the phone at arm's length from my body, wondering what I had just heard. I was stunned and confused. I put the phone back to my ear and said, "Sweetheart, I have no opinion about whether you and Greg should have a third child. That's too personal for me to have an opinion about."

She persisted. "Dad, don't tell me that. You have an opinion about everything. Just please tell me what you think."

Again, I was baffled. I responded, "Sweetheart, I really trust the combined opinion of you and Greg, and I have no personal opinion or preference. If you choose to have a third child, that's fine by me. If you choose not to have a third child, that's fine by me."

She replied sweetly, "Thanks, Dad," and she hung up. Was she sincerely grateful that I expressed confidence in her opinion, or was she being dismissive?

For me, that scene was totally ambiguous. It still is. Did I say the "right" thing? I really don't know. My point is crystal clear. We never know when "suddenly" will happen, and there is no way to be prepared for anything and everything, although we must be prudent, proactive, and planning. Again, the paradox of ambiguity. Again, the claim that all is well.

By the way, Beth and Greg did have a third child, their first girl, Kaitlyn. That was nine years ago. Suffice it to say, little Kaitlyn is a sheer gift from God.

Father Hopko used to say, "If a person wants to be sure of the road that he or she is traveling on, then they must close their eyes and travel in the dark."

I learned this lesson well from my wife throughout our marriage of nineteen years. She had an artistic soul and was deeply intuitive. Towards the end of her life she was diagnosed with metastatic bone cancer. The oncologist said, "Bone cancer is the most painful of all cancers, but you won't die from it. You'll die from something else." She did. She died of heart failure. Her bone cancer was so painful that morphine didn't touch the pain. She was traveling in the dark, and she traveled courageously.

Authentic Wellness Requires Conflict

WE HAVE THE WORDS of St. John Chrysostom, "Do not fear conflict and do not flee from it. Where there is no struggle, there is no virtue; where faith and love are not tempted, it is not possible to be sure that they are really present. They are proved and revealed in adversity."

"Life is difficult," is the opening line of a powerful book, *The Road Less Traveled*, by M. Scott Peck. Over the years I have considered those simple words and find them to be an accurate summary of the human life saga—but a serious understatement. Life is immensely messy and incredibly unpredictable. Stuff happens! We might well wonder, "Does life have to be this difficult?" The unvarnished truth is that life is difficult to the point of being absurd. Jesus, who is God Almighty, died on a cross. M. Scott Peck, who wrote the insightful words under discussion, is dead. Death awaits us all. The absurdity is boundless.

And therein resides our unbounded hope. Therein resides the calmness of fire, the fierce calmness. Christ died on a cross, precisely to save us from absurdity. Life is paradoxical. We know we will die, yet we live joyfully inside the kingdom of love, here and now. And after we die, we expect to live in the kingdom of love forever. Unfathomable. I would say that daily life is an immense spiritual warfare, the size of which we can easily underestimate, at our own risk.

"Satan is real," Father Alexander Schmemann would often remind young seminarians. He would also add that Satan isn't hanging around at 42nd Street in New York City. Satan has already conquered much of that vicinity. Rather, Father Schmemann would conclude that Satan and his legion are roaming the fourteen acres of Saint Vladimir's Seminary to seductively capture our souls.

In my own experience, I find that my life is a continuous unseen spiritual warfare. On the outside, my relationships and projects are relatively balanced and stable. On the inside, my mind is often chaotic and turbulent, for a multitude of reasons. I refer to my mental upset in old-fashioned terms, such as a "mumbo-jumbo" mindset. The warfare is intense, and the variations on the theme of temptations are too numerous to count.

Sometimes the inner world seems utterly dark and gloomy, even when the sun shines brightly outside. The experience is rather like being in a forest at midnight without any light, moonless and defenseless.

The story is told that when Satan is preparing young demons, he tells them that their most potent weapon is to get humans to believe that he, Satan, is not real. In our culture there is a tendency to minimize the horror, the savage influence of Satan. He is often portrayed as a red semihuman with a tail and a pitchfork. We name sports teams "Devils," as a friendly mascot. All this tragically enhances the unearthly power Satan and his legionnaires can wield over us.

A young college graduate sent me an email that I cherish. She wrote, "I feel like a speck looking up at a great high mountain ahead of me. I am so small, so tiny, so easily lost and so incredibly weak, yet precious and eternally significant in the sight of my Savior. I worship Him and that is all that matters. I relate to the psalmist in saying he is a worm. We are all worms, and Christ carries us up the mountain."

Unrelenting Warfare

ONE METAPHOR for the human mind is a lake in the woods. The surface of the lake changes with the weather. Some days the surface is placid and serene. Some days the surface is raucous with waves that could topple a canoe. Some days the surface is frozen solid. Below the surface, at mid-level, the water is more stabilized. At the bottom of the lake, the water is calm and unchanging. That's my own experience. Much of the time I have intense surface-of-the-lake mental warfare. At the same time I have a deep peace about it all, aware that Christ is doing for me what I can't do for myself.

I remember my dreams rather often. These episodes occur in the middle of the night. Last night I slept for a couple of hours, then awoke and was awake for two and a half hours. The warfare was unrelenting. Sometime during the night, I dreamed that I conversed with a colleague about a serious matter. Much of the temptation was about one-upmanship—about me being right and showing him how right I was. As I became more awake, I knew the ideas were from the dark side, so I was able to pray each time I was aware of the tempting thoughts.

Some nights the temptations are about illicit pleasures that seem so enticing. When I am awake, I feel the nighttime experiences are almost tactile. I can instantly feel shamed and guilty for something I didn't do, didn't want to do, and don't want to do. Those upsetting temptations are not only night episodes. My daytime can be marked by unexpected and violent temptations of various sorts. Daydreams of sorts. But God does give me the grace to pray when I am aware of these thoughts, which are basically lies.

The classic of Orthodox ascetic literature *Unseen Warfare* makes these points clearly. I would recommend the book for serious Christian seekers. My basic point in my little book is that we need to continually adjust our expectations. As St. Paul says in 1 Corinthians, "[He] will not allow you to be tempted beyond what you are able, but with the temptation will also make the way of escape, that you may be able to bear *it*" (1 Cor. 10:13).

But we must also know that resisting temptation is exhausting and, for some of us, nearly impossible at times, especially for addicts. We can try to remain calm in the midst of mental strife. We can try to live with our basic attitude at the bottom of the lake, all the while living in the real world with its real stressors. We can repeat, without fully comprehending, "All is well."

The story is told of St. Teresa of Avila, the Roman Catholic mystic who was instrumental in the establishment of the Discalced Carmelites. After establishing a large mother house for her nuns, she decided to spread the order by organizing a daughter house some miles away. She selected a few nuns, and they set off in a horse-drawn carriage. They descended a slight hill to cross a creek, and in the creek, a wheel came off the carriage. All the nuns got out, rolled up their sleeves and the bottom of their habits, and began to repair the carriage—changing the tire, so to speak.

The weather in Spain that day was very hot, and the mosquitoes were relentless in their attack upon the perspiring nuns. The scene was rather gruesome. At one point, Teresa raised her fist to the sky and said loudly, "God, if this is the way you treat your friends, no wonder you have so few."

Her conflict was relentless, yet she persisted in her faith. Life for even the greatest of saints was filled with ambiguity.

Premature Closure

EARLY IN MY CAREER as a high school guidance counselor, I had a supervisor who occasionally confided in me. He was stout and had a red face. One day he called me into his office to say he had gone to see his cardiologist, who told him that because he had a history of early heart attacks in his family and his blood pressure was quite high, he must stop drinking alcohol. My supervisor was visibly upset.

I asked, "What are you going to do?"

He looked at me as if I had asked a totally stupid question. He said, "Of course, I am going to get a different doctor."

Don't we all have a tendency to deny some parts of reality, as suits our perceptions? Don't we all find reality too much of a burden to endure, and resort to one or another mental dodge or defensive mechanism? For our purposes we can call this *premature closure*, that is, a solution that has virtually no plausibility in reality. I knew my supervisor well enough to know that, deep down, he knew that his response was counterintuitive. As we can see, ambiguity is easy to resolve with premature closure, but the price is high.

I might ask you, the reader, to pause and ask yourself what are the ambiguities in your life now. I do this at parish retreats. The discussion that follows is a help to the others who are there because we can often identify with the struggles of others.

Sometimes we can feel overwhelmed by our ambiguities. What to do? The crisp, clear answer is to try to simply say, "Lord have mercy" and have a cup of tea. Saint Irenaeus tells us to "relax in God's hands." Simple but not always easy.

CHAPTER 3

Where Is Heaven?

A GAIN WE RETURN to the wondrous truth that Orthodoxy is paradoxy. Heaven is both a place where the righ-
teous go after they die, and heaven is now, ever-present in our
hearts where the Lord dwells. So heaven is a paradox. Heaven
is, yet is not yet. Heaven is here, and heaven is forthcoming.

We can conclude that heaven is not a place "up there" somewhere. Heaven is not hidden above the clouds. Rather than saying heaven is "up," we can say that heaven is "in," in our deepest
heart. "It is no longer I who live, but Christ lives in me" (Gal.
2:20). Christ is the embodiment of heaven. But we often miss
the beauty and the majesty of heaven in the present moment,
especially in moments of high stress.

Heaven Is Where All Is Well

IF HEAVEN IS WITHIN MY HEART, then it is not a Herculean
leap to conclude, "All is well." But, although we humans know

that with our minds, we easily forget who we are and what is really going on.

One way to ponder heaven is to ponder Christ. Orthodox Christianity is an incarnational theology in the best sense of the word, as is demonstrated clearly by our church architecture. Many Orthodox churches have a large icon of Christ as Pantocrator, the embracer of all in the universe, high above the nave in the center of the church. The emphasis is upon Christ's presence within our world, within our church, within us, His immanence.

By contrast, many Western churches have beautiful high towers and spires that emphasize the "upness" of Christ, the transcendence of the Holy One. Neither architecture is right or wrong, better or lesser. The architecture is simply different. Christ, like heaven, is both transcendent and immanent. Orthodoxy embraces both of Christ's manifestations, but it might be fair to say that Orthodoxy folds the transcendent into the immanent.

As a non-Orthodox child, I was taught to fold my hands flat together, pointed upward, to send my prayers "up" to God. This was especially important when children received the Eucharist. We Orthodox teach our children to cross their arms and hands as they receive the Eucharist, to indicate a desire to have God inside them. There is no conflict between transcendence and immanence, but there can be a distinct difference in emphasis.

God is transcendent, beyond our wildest dreams. He is

making zebras and mosquitoes. He is giving us breath and focusing the retinas of our eyes. Yet He is so immanent, so small, that He "fits" inside the Eucharist.

Heaven is earth transformed by love when we live the life of love; the suffering of earth is transformed into a foretaste of heaven when we move guided by the inner center of love. The point is that heaven is earth transformed in our life, here and now. Our peaceful breath is our heavenly experience.

As Up, So Down

IN HEAVEN, the bruises of suffering will not be eliminated but will be transformed by divine love into a newness of life. Christ's risen body still carries the nail prints and scars of His crucifixion. Heaven is not a place of eternal slumber or a long sleep-in, but a life of constant change, continual creativity and newness, changing from glory to glory, more into Christ.

St. Anthony the Great tells us, "The fruits of the earth are not brought to perfection immediately, but by time, rain, and care; similarly, the fruits of men ripen through ascetic practice, study, time, perseverance, self-control, and patience." As I read and reread this quote, I am struck by the precision of the phrase "but by time, rain, and care."

There are many questions inside me that pivot on the question of heaven and nonheaven, sometimes called hell. Dostoyevsky said that hell is an absence of love. Hell is not the painted fiery river into which we are thrown to scream for all eternity. Hell is an absence of love, whatever that means. My questions about heaven are multiple and varied. Will I know my wife as a woman/wife/endearing person? Will I be able to know Christ as a friend? What was Jesus' adolescence like? Did the Theotokos have pain at childbirth? When I discuss these questions with theologians I get differing answers. That's one good reason that I look forward to heaven, as an opportunity to meet Christ face-to-face and to get answers.

What is clear is that we have a choice. We can choose one side or the other, because heaven and earth are both inside of us right now, and it's our choice that determines just where we will reside in the current moment, now. I'm free.

I would add that our freedom can be limited by our own choices. When we make dark choices, we can change the way we think and thereby become locked into dark thought patterns, limiting our freedom. We sometimes choose kindness, goodness, compassion, love, and sometimes we just choose to be self-centered, neglectful, shadowy, and perhaps even cruel. So it's all about consciousness. What are we conscious *of*, light or darkness?

One thing is for sure. If I spend a great deal of time pondering the front page of any daily newspaper or the evening news on TV, and if I keep thinking about it, wondering about it, worrying about the future and the way we seem to be preparing to destroy ourselves—all of that ugliness has to do with *me*. We

each have much more control over our thoughts than we sometimes believe. I am not enslaved to my thoughts.

Cure for Loneliness

VIRTUALLY EVERYONE has bouts of loneliness. Being lonely
does not seem to be a foretaste of heaven. Some of us are lonely
most of the time, unmarried and married. Some of us are rarely
lonely. We all differ according to our social needs.

It has been said that the cure for loneliness is solitude—
because we are never truly alone, without Christ. Of course, ini-
tially solitude can bring up darkness, but if we live through it, we
can be "in heaven," so to speak. We can, to some extent, try to be
in the presence of Christ who lives within us and be "in heaven."

The Heart of the Matter

SINCE HEAVEN IS WITHIN, how do we get to the heaven
within? St. Isaac the Syrian says, "Enter eagerly into the treasure house that is within you and you will find the things that
are of heaven."

The heart of the matter is our heart, and examining our
thoughts gives us access to our heart. We can change our
thoughts and therefore change our entire being. St. Theophan
the Recluse tells us our heart is our home. Or, as some say,
wherever you are, that is your home.

Early in our marriage, as we approached my birthday, my wife said to me, "Al, what do you want from me for your birthday?"

I said, "You are my wife and you are asking me what I want from you for my birthday. Well, OK, I'll tell you. Many of the things in life that I want I don't get, and that's all right. What I would like from you is a birthday card with a note that says I have a weekend at the upstate monastery, leaving from the university at three o'clock on Friday afternoon and returning at eight-thirty on Sunday evening. But you work as a nurse and are raising two children. I know that such a request is beyond a reasonable expectation, but you asked."

For my birthday I received a card that said I could spend a weekend at the monastery, and that she would like a little notice so she could plan ahead. I went to the monastery for the weekend and returned at eight-thirty Sunday evening. A half hour later, my wife hugged me and said, "Al, I want you to go to the monastery every weekend of our marriage. This is the Al I married. I treasure you when you are this way."

Solitude and prayer have an uplifting effect on my psyche. Of course, I didn't go to the monastery every weekend of our marriage, but I did receive a birthday gift for such a weekend every year for many years to come.

The Present Moment

WHAT ARE THE DETAILS of my present moment? This moment? This minimoment? I'll begin with a rather astounding claim: This present moment is the best moment of my life. Why would I say that? Because the present moment is the only point of contact I have with God. All else, past and future, is a construct of my imagination. The present moment is the only reality I have.

Dr. Ann Bezzerides, director of the Office of Vocation and Ministry at Hellenic College, wrote the following lines to college students: "Here's the thing—to invite Christ into daily life and decisions, big and little, is to feel the weight of the future lifted." She goes on to say that we (the college students) can never "miss'" our vocation, because our vocation is always now. Our vocation is to invite Christ into our lives, now.

The present moment is not an endless series of still photographs, one after another, static and frozen in time. Rather, the present moment is a liquid, flowing, seamless experience. What metaphor can we use? None is adequate, but let's try the waves on the ocean. The waves move and undulate, smooth and rough, but always in symmetrical motion. We might say that our experience of the present moment is that of being a wave on the ocean, sometimes evident and sometimes almost hidden, but always a living movement as part of a larger context. The present moment is, for us, an invitation to be abandoned to the movement of the winds, the ocean current, and the gravitational forces of the planet.

Of course, every moment varies and is unique. For me, the details of my present moment often include some dose of anxiety, mild or moderate. I don't seem to have much mental space for a purely serene, anxiety-free present moment. OK. That's me. All I can do with the complexity of the present moment is surrender it with a nod, which is my personal code for the word "Jesus," which is code for "the Jesus Prayer." Most of the time I don't even nod. I simply become aware of the details—the sights, sounds, and tactile sensations—of the present moment, my current breath. And that's enough. I don't have to do mental gymnastics to try to do "more," to make some prayer or special awareness of the presence of God within the present moment. No. Prayer is fine when appropriate. Silence is fine when appropriate. Awareness of the details of the present moment can be, in itself, prayer if preceded by a faith in Christ's presence within me.

Expectations for the Present Moment

MIGHT I EXPECT MYSELF to be serene most of the time? Heavens, no. At least, that is not my experience. What can we say about that? When I am aware that I am not serene, but off-center, then I come back to an awareness of my breath, perhaps for a couple of breaths. I breathe gently, a bit deeper and a bit slower. That's it. Does this bring serenity? Not necessarily, but it does bring me into an awareness of the present moment.

The present moment is elusive. In the Twelve Step movements there is a wonderful slogan to help members to give up their egos: the member is told to do "the next right thing." Such an attitude takes away the anxiety of ego-drivenness. Yet, like most of human experience, such an attitude is paradoxical. For me, "doing the next right thing" is not helpful. Why? "Doing the next right thing" often prompts me to live in an awareness of the next right thing, upcoming, and not in the present moment. Lord, have mercy.

Seek Stillness

STILLNESS WON'T SEEK US. We must seek her. She can be elusive, mysterious, and uncomfortable. She doesn't resist us. We resist her. It is charming to think of silence as feminine. In classical mythology the feminine is portrayed as receptive. Silence is primarily receptive.

During the summers of my childhood, I would often sit on the porch swing with my dad, beneath the oversized tin roof. We enjoyed the cool evening breeze while saying very little. Most of the time we said nothing. We sat like that because my dad often asked me to "sit" with him awhile. After some time of pleasant silence, my dad would simply say, "Thank you," which meant that I could go play. Do we have the courage to ask someone else to sit on a porch swing, or wherever, just to sit awhile?

God commissioned His people to seek stillness. At the Passover the Egyptians were hotly pursuing the Israelites to kill them. God said, in effect, my job is to fight for you and eliminate your enemies. He said, "the Egyptians whom you see today, you will never see again. [I] will fight for you" (Ex 14:13, 14). Your job is to allow me to do that for you. Immediately after this, Yahweh told the Israelites precisely what He wanted of them: He told Moses to tell the people, "you shall hold your peace" (Ex 14:14).

Psalm 46 states, "Be still, and know that I am God" (Ps 46:11 RSV). The converse is implied: if I am not still, I may not know God. And if I don't know God, I am not going to know myself, because I am made in His image and likeness. As a clinical psychologist, I have seen many persons for therapy, from all walks of life. The common thread is a lack of peace, a lack of inner calmness, a lack of centered identity. Most of these persons don't have stillness or calmness in their lives. Most of my clients don't have a personal sense of being made in God's image and likeness.

If we begin to seek stillness, to meditate, what can we expect? We can expect inner trouble. If we sit for a set period of time, the first set of things to cross our mind is likely to be all our incomplete tasks, like, "Oh, I need to call my sister," or, "Ugh, I haven't finished my prep for my upcoming presentation." But these uncomfortable thoughts will pass, and then we might settle into more of an awareness of our breath and a short repetitive prayer. We are likely to have distractions all along the way. That's OK.

For many of us, stillness appears to be too hard to do, too much to try. We prefer to be busy, even busy doing "good" things. When I give parish retreats, I continue to be surprised by the responses when I teach about sitting in silence. I tell them that Father Hopko, in his Fifty-Five Maxims of the Christian Life, recommends that we sit in silence twenty to thirty minutes each day. I ask the participants to begin with five or ten minutes and work up to twenty to thirty minutes a day.

The surprise happens when I meet them again a year later and ask how they are doing with their silent sitting. Many will say something like, "I need to start on Monday." OK, but there is a high price to pay for avoiding intentional quiet time with the Lord.

I can't resist sharing an excerpt from an email I received from a seventeen-year-old boy who attended CrossRoad, a summer institute at Hellenic College for high school students. At this institute, I asked the participants to meditate daily for five minutes. I asked them to sit quietly with a timer, gently be aware of their breathing, say a soft repetitive prayer inwardly, and try not to think of anything else. Of course, distractions will abound.

A couple of months later I received this boy's email. In essence, he said:

I was wondering how to progress in silence. I remember you said that you personally take forty minutes every day to be silent. I have been silent every day these last three and a half, almost four weeks, since getting out of CrossRoad, except for a day or two where I forgot. I have set a timer for five minutes, and at the end of it, I usually continue to be silent for a few minutes more. I have this feeling that what I'm doing is not enough. I was wondering, when would you suggest I increase the amount of time I am silent every day? After several months? Is there a specific time increment we should be increasing by?

I simply responded that he should proceed slowly and talk it over with his spiritual father or confessor. I also told him that the process is about a relationship with Christ. We don't force prayer, yet we follow a regular prayer rule. You and I can learn a great deal from this boy's desire for Christ in the form of daily silence.

The Breath of Life

AS ST. IGNATIUS BRIANCHANINOV instructs us, "We breathe with care, gently and slowly." He adds that attention to the present moment can be aided by "quiet, steady breathing." When we are anxious, our breathing is shallow. Quiet, steady breathing can be anti-anxiety breathing, an antidepressant of sorts.

St. Irenaeus said, "Relax in God's hands." I think it would be appropriate to also say, "Relax in God's breath." God's *ruach*, breath, is our breath. We don't breathe ourselves. We are breathed by God's very own breath.

Our breath is our entry into our heart. When we are attentive to our breathing, we can become centered more easily. Then, with attention, we can take the next step. As Robert Frost wrote, "Live life like it is the last breath you take, for that breath is the whole essence of living, the little things in life are what connects us to all the big things we live for."

I need to learn much more, and probably you do too. I need to learn that God does speak to us, and that it's a matter of awareness, however God chooses to make His presence and His voice known. But we can be assured that His light does come into and through to us. This can be our path to heaven as we understand the word.

CHAPTER 4

All Is Pure

....

ONE OF THE BEATITUDES SAYS, "Blessed *are* the pure in heart, / For they shall see God" (Matt. 5:8). This beatitude seems to contain two hidden implications. First, the pure in heart shall see God on this earth, not merely in the hereafter. Second, the converse is implied—if we are not pure of heart, we might not see God in our lifetime.

We know that we don't become pure by our own efforts. Rather, purity is a gift that we can accept or refuse. We can till the soil to make ourselves more receptive to the grace of purity, but, like the gardener who tills the soil, we can't make the flowers grow.

Impure persons struggle for wellness. Jesus said that we are to clothe the naked. Those persons who are given to lustful activity try to do the opposite, that is, to make naked those who are clothed, if only in the lustful person's mind. And, of course, most of us are a mixture of purity and impurity—at least, of impurities of mind or behavior in our past.

St. Athanasius of Alexandria said, "You cannot put straight

in others what is warped in yourself." If we are to have some healing influence upon others, we need to first become pure ourselves.

We are told in the epistle to Titus, "To the pure all things are pure" (Titus 1:15). That is a bold claim, because the word used is "all." We might conclude that "all is well" for the pure of heart, or at least those who want to be pure of heart, tempted though they may be.

We can witness purity of heart and learn from the innocence of children. Once my five-year-old granddaughter Kaitlyn, whom I've called Angel for her entire lifetime, asked me to come into her room. When we arrived I said, "Angel, what's up?"

She said, "Poppa, my wing hurts."

I said, "I didn't know that a wing could hurt."

She replied, "Oh, sure, Poppa, my wing is like my arm. If I bang my wing against a wall, it gets bruised." So we spent some time putting imaginary bandages on her imaginary wing. She was old enough to know that she doesn't have wings, yet young enough to make up a delightful make-believe game that she and her Poppa could play together, based on her nickname. During this interaction I knew that our thoughts were innocent, playful, creative, and uplifting. This was a moment—like others we have shared—for both of us to treasure. For me, this is purity demonstrated. Purity is about cleanliness of heart, spotlessness of the mind.

Inner Purity of Heart

ST. ISAAC THE SYRIAN says that it is better to acquire purity of heart than to convert whole nations from error. According to Metropolitan Kallistos Ware, these words of St. Isaac mean that unless and until we have gained some measure of inner silence, it is improbable that we will really succeed in converting anybody to anything. We acquire purity of heart by more quiet prayer.

Purity of heart requires a certain kind of effort. The effort is delicate, not like a New Year's resolution. Purity of heart has more to do with yielding than striving. Purity is something the Lord does through us as we freely want to pray, to be prayed through. In a sense, we pray and the Lord prays through us.

The visible world is our entry into the invisible world. The inner universe, the invisible world, is much larger than the visible. This is the mystery of incarnation, the mystery of Christ becoming flesh and living as flesh through us.

On our wedding day, Galina and I pondered and discussed the statement, "Every human person is a mystery that must be learned slowly, reverently, with care and tenderness and pain, and is never learned completely." We knew that, with effort, everything could be well for us. We had two children during our nineteen-year marriage while she was alive on this planet. We are still married, although she has been in heaven for more than twenty-five years.

Purity Is a Choice

I AM CURRENTLY SEEING a young man for counseling who has problems with his passions. I have changed some of the details to protect his anonymity. He is a professor who is engaged to an attractive woman whom he loves dearly, and who loves him. During a class at a university, the professor noticed that a very pretty female student was smitten by him. When the course was finished and the grades given, there was no more professor-student ethical constraint. The professor then called the student, met with her, and they had sexual intercourse. When it was finished, the student said, "I feel like the cat that swallowed the canary." The professor was silently smug in response to her comment. He felt that he had satisfied her, and that she was a happy camper. However, he had no intention of ever seeing her again. He intended to marry his fiancée.

On his drive home, he said, he stopped and had a hamburger with tomato, lettuce, onion, and ketchup. He said the thought occurred to him that the best part of the night was the hamburger. He didn't yet understand that sex without love is empty and unfulfilling. He also didn't comprehend the profound truth in his student's comment—he was the "canary" that she had swallowed. He had given her part of his very soul, his identity. Mistakenly, he thought that he had seduced her and that they had had a mutually erotic time together, end of story. He didn't realize that is not the way life works. As St. Paul says, "Or do you not know that he who is joined to a harlot is one body with her? For 'the two,' He says, 'shall become one flesh'" (1 Cor. 6:16). Of course, the admonition pertains not only to prostitutes but to anyone who is not one's wife or husband.

A few weeks later, the student called the professor to ask him to accompany her on a short vacation to the Bahamas. He said to himself that he couldn't have been less interested. He had gotten what he wanted from her. He gently made an excuse and never heard from her again. He said that he slowly began to feel guilty because of what he had done. Purity is a choice.

I had an opportunity to choose purity when my daughter, Beth, and I took a trip to Greece for ten days. Beth had recently graduated college and didn't have enough money to go anywhere for a vacation. Going to Greece with her dad seemed like a fine enough substitute for something more exotic. I explained to her that I intended to "monastery hop," that is, visit monasteries and not do the vacationland Greek isles. She was fine with that.

After eight days of interesting visits to Thessaloniki and various monasteries, I decided to give Beth a day off. I told her she could do whatever she wanted, which was to swim in the crystal blue water of the Aegean. I had read in the visitor's guide that beaches in Greece were topless unless marked "family beach." She chose a beach that was beautiful but unmarked. I said she could swim and sunbathe all day while I would sit on a bench near the car and read a book.

Beth got quite angry. "What's wrong? I did all you wanted. You can swim. Why won't you swim with me?" I hemmed and hawed. Beth persisted. "Just tell me why you won't swim with me."

I replied, "OK, Sweetheart, I'll tell you why. This beach is topless, and I prefer not to go."

Beth got angrier. "I won't be topless. I have a one-piece swimsuit." She became philosophical. "Are you against museums that have statues of nude women?"

I said, "I respect beautiful statues of women in museums. I just don't want to go to this beach today."

Off she went in a huff. Two and a half hours later she hadn't come back, and I decided that I had better check that the hot sun hadn't overcome her. I walked to where she was. There was no one else on the beach. Lying on her back, with sufficient sunscreen, she looked up and we talked. Then I heard a car park behind me and people come down to the beach where we were. I couldn't see them. They lay down on towels right behind where I stood.

In a sweet voice Beth said, "Dad, I have a request. Please don't turn around."

I said, "Thanks, Sweetheart," and I backed away so I didn't have to look at the people behind me, probably topless women. I didn't want to be a puritan or set a policy for Beth. I simply did not want to be in the company of topless women.

So all is pure for those who seek purity because God always

provides a way out. Being at a beach with topless women might be OK for some people, but not for me. That's all I know.

Lust and Anger

ST. MAXIMUS THE CONFESSOR makes the point that lust and anger are similar passions. Both come from a deeper pool of inner passion. He says that a person who is angry may very well have a lust issue, and vice versa. As a psychologist, I try to make the most of this foundational insight. That is, if I see a person, usually a man, who is regularly angry, I wonder if he is addicted to pornography. Sometimes I am right, sometimes I am wrong, but it is a hypothesis worth pondering.

As I think about anger, I recall my experiences with angry people. When I was a young adult, I marched in anti-war rallies in Washington, DC. On one occasion I went with my wife. I knew there was a possibility the marchers would be sprayed with mace. Mace hurts. The eyes swell, and the body gets itchy. I asked my wife to sit in our Volkswagen in a safe neighborhood so she wouldn't get hurt, and so she could drive us back to New York. During the rally I was mildly hit by mace. My eyes burned and I felt stressed. I also knew that there was much lustful activity among the young protesters, but I could overlook that in the name of justice and the ending of what seemed an unjust war (the war in Vietnam).

My experience was, at best, mixed. Some of the angriest

people I ever met were behind the bullhorns, shouting inflammatory words at the crowd. I felt humiliated by being associated with such adversarial rhetoric. The leaders behind the bullhorns were bullying the crowd. I knew the leaders were doing exactly the opposite of what I had hoped. That was the last anti-war, anti-government rally I ever approved or went to.

For me, there is a significant difference between the quiet prayer vigils protesting an imminent death sentence and some anti-war protests. Oh yes, some of the saintliest people I ever met were in the peace movement, but they were quiet and restrained.

I must also admit that I met some Orthodox persons in the peace movement who adamantly disagreed with me. I once gave a talk entitled "Peace and Purity" to a large group. During the talk I mentioned my anti-war experience. A small but vocal portion of the group approached me afterwards and badgered me. They angrily said I was wrong and that I should fight for what is just. They said that we need to use anger, because that is the only language the government understands. They said that we must speak the government's language to have a voice.

I said I have a different opinion. I don't think we need to play on their playing field. There is too much anger. Personally, after thirty years of thinking about the peace movements, I am convinced that some peaceniks have done as much moral damage as war hawks in days gone by. I have also heard it said that the terrorists of tomorrow are the fierce peaceniks of today. Maybe so.

Lust Contaminates Purity

WE LIVE in a sex-saturated culture. That is the way it is. Father John Breck, in his book, *The Sacred Gift of Life*, said, "Our threshold of tolerance toward sexual explicitness and exploitation has been dramatically lowered . . . and . . . the spiritual and psychological toll extracted by this situation is incalculable." We can become numb to the devastating consequences of lustful comments and behaviors.

We all have a long way to go to become pure of heart. We are called to be pure as the driven snow, pure as the feeling we have after taking a shower with Irish Spring soap. Since we are already contaminated by sin, the task is to allow God to remove the impurities.

Purity of mind and heart transcends sexuality. That is, it is about more than the mere presence or absence of sexual attraction. But it must be cultivated. Perhaps we can begin by examining our entertainment standards. What we do with our leisure time says much about foundational values. How do we use our leisure? Our leisure activities may uncover some of our hidden demons. Hidden demons can be consciously concealed from others and even unconsciously hidden from ourselves. We can be oblivious to their existence, as we might be to a latent deadly virus in our bloodstream.

It took me a long while to finally establish my own entertainment plan. I don't try to impose my standards on my children or my students. But I do my best to live by them. I will not watch any nudity or sex on TV, in movies, or on my computer. That's it. My children know my standards. When they went off to college, they were on their own and watched what they chose to watch. I didn't ask them because I knew I was no longer capable of controlling their leisure. Interestingly, on different occasions each adult child would say, "Dad, I have a movie to recommend that even you can see." They referred to those movies as "Dad-proof," not unlike "bulletproof," for purity reasons.

More than ever we need authentic elders in our culture. Some teachers have given up the role and choose to act rather like teens. The news media carried a story of a high school teacher who began a legal battle to be able to attend the senior prom with one of her students. Her case was built on individual rights and the power to express herself however she wants.

Our culture, our Church, needs elders, not merely older people, who show our youth a different set of values, even if the youth can't adopt those values fully right away. My children now have children, and they seem to be as strict with their children as I was with them. They are becoming elders in their own way.

I know a high school girl whose great desire in life is to watch the Victoria's Secret Fashion Show. The girl doesn't yet know that such desires can end up causing her much pain, but for now, she is adamant in her impulses. Her parents don't see much wrong with the girl's desires. They say that she will "grow out of it." Perhaps, but the price might be high.

Overcoming Lustful Temptations

SOMETIMES THOUGHTS OF LUST can seem almost tactile, that is, almost real. Sometimes lustful thoughts can be so vivid that the person who is tempted might feel as if he or she had done what the temptation suggested, even though he or she didn't give in to the temptation. Satan is cunning, baffling, and powerful, and it is important to make a clear distinction between temptation and sin. This distinction is vital.

Sometimes we are tempted by thoughts of wild, scummy images. Those thoughts are not sin. If we are tempted by luscious, attractive images, that is not sin. Those thoughts don't make us dirty old men or women. No, those thoughts are temptations. The moment we become aware of our thoughts, that is the moment of truth. If we relinquish the thoughts in prayer or simply turn to something else, that constitutes victory. If, however, we indulge those thoughts and magnify them, then that is sin. It is no sin to be tempted sorely.

An Orthodox Jewish rabbi told me, "When I get a serious lust temptation I know it is God speaking to me. God is saying, 'I am here with you. Let's conquer this temptation together.'"

We are called to quell and redirect the energy of lust into vigorous, pure thoughts. We are called to conquer lustful thoughts by actively surrendering the thoughts to the Lord. In this way we exert a "muscular Christianity," as was said of St. Anthony when he went into the desert to "fight the demons," namely the demons of *logismoi*, or thoughts.

St. Anthony said that in the desert he experienced victory over temptations of the eyes, the ears, and the mouth because there was nothing to see, hear, or speak to. He said there was only one temptation left for the man in the desert, the temptation of *porneia*. St. Anthony's temptations, or *porneia*, were not about live, flesh-and-blood women. There were no beauty queens in the desert knocking at his door for a loaf of bread. No, the temptations of *porneia* were in his head, in his thoughts, put there by the demons he had set out to fight. And Satan was difficult to recognize; usually he looked like the things Anthony missed most.

When Anthony emerged, he asked the Lord where He had been for all those years. Apparently the Lord said, "I was here but I would see and abide to see thy battle, and because thou hast manly fought and well maintained thy battle, I shall make thy name to be spread through all the world."

Amma Sarah, a saintly desert mother, had a similar experience. She said that she was tempted for thirteen years by thoughts of *porneia*. She did not ask that the temptations be removed. Instead she asked for victory over them, and God granted her request. Amma Sarah experienced the same basic temptations as St. Anthony, as is true for many of us.

Matter Matters

OUR OUTER WORLD and its inner significance can come together to create wholeness and sanctity. The result is deep joy and a sense of radiant beauty. The Incarnation of Jesus showed us that matter is, and always has been, *the hiding place for Spirit,* forever offering itself to be discovered anew. Matter matters.

Eve is called God's finishing touch in creation. Eve embodies the beauty and the mystery and the tender vulnerability of God. She also embodies the immovable strength of a woman. The Theotokos, as the new Eve, shows us the perfect living example of a caring, strong, nurturing, and pure woman in every regard. She was not a revered beauty queen in her day. We have no evidence that she preferred elegant luxuries. She did not appear on the cover of the Jewish manuscripts, or whatever the equivalent of that would have been in her time. She did not allow her outer or inner beauty to be exploited. Yet she is the loveliest woman ever, and ever shall be.

The way men regard the female body is a living paradox. On the one hand, a woman's body is the temple of God, the gift of love to her husband in marriage, and a source of life for her infant. Paradoxically, on the other hand, her body can be photographed for internet pornography or sold for money in prostitution.

The same paradox holds for a male body, but differently. The female and male bodies are equal, but different. In fact, some biologists tell us that men and women are different in every cell of the body. The poet William Blake said, "The naked woman's body is a portion of eternity too great for the eye of man." Again, this is a paradox.

Orthodox Christians believe that sex is created by God and is very good, but so good that it is only sacred in a monogamous, heterosexual marriage. Sex requires an eternal, loving context. Orthodox Christians are not like the Puritans, who taught that sex is inherently bad and would not talk about it. The Orthodox vision sees sex within marriage as an intimate, sacred, and, at times, robust act of loving another person as a foretaste of heaven.

Just as an aside, celibate persons can attain a similar foretaste of heaven without sexual activity. Sexual activity is created that we may learn to love as Christ loves. Celibate persons can learn to love as Christ loves without marital sex. The celibate life is different from married life, neither better nor worse. By God's providence, it is simply a different path.

But it is also true that lust can easily creep into the marital bed. It is possible for us as children of Adam and Eve to be thinking of someone else while making love to our marital partner, or simply to imagine that more is happening than really is.

There are some persons who, because of nature or nurture or both, have strong same-sex attraction. That sensitive topic is beyond the scope of this little book. Suffice it to say that all persons are called to strive for purity as best they can so the beatitude comes true for them in this lifetime.

Matter matters, and we are free to transform and transfigure matter into a new transparent image of God in this human life. For those who are seeking purity of heart, the truth that "all is well" can become more a part of our experience, more alive, and more tangible in everyday joys and challenges. Remember, as St. Paul says in the Epistle to Titus, "To the pure all things are pure." To the pure, colors are more vibrant, sounds more melodic, and life more exhilarating.

CHAPTER 5

Our Weakness Is Our Strength

VERY FIBER IN MY BEING resists the truth that in my weakness is my strength. All of me seems to want a "muscular Christianity," for men and for women. But I also know that a muscular Christianity begins with a stark admission of powerlessness, of utter weakness.

We know all too clearly what St. Paul says in 2 Corinthians:

> And [the Lord] said to me, "My grace is sufficient for you, for My strength is made perfect in weakness." Therefore most gladly I will rather boast in my infirmities, that the power of Christ may rest upon me. Therefore I take pleasure in infirmities, in reproaches, in needs, in persecutions, in distresses, for Christ's sake. For when I am weak, then I am strong. (2 Cor. 12:9, 10)

Yes, we know the Lord's way, yet we can find much difficulty in incorporating the truth into our personal lives.

Close Brush with Death

WHEN I WAS YOUNGER, I often went kayaking and loved it. Once I visited Pittsburgh and decided to stop at Point Park, a park where the three rivers meet. I was born and raised in Pittsburgh, so the trip had an air of déjà vu about it. I rented a kayak on a pleasant day. I saw a family in two rented kayaks, the father and mother in one and the two teen children in the other.

I knew there were "suck holes" in the Allegheny River, caused by dredging the bottom of the river for sand, leaving a hole in the bottom that forced the water to swirl downward. Near the top of the river, though not visible, was a fatal whirlpool that had taken the lives of teenage boys who were swimming in the river. I knew a couple of those boys when I was a teenager. I also knew that there was a dam a few miles down the river, where a kayak could not safely maneuver. But I saw the family kayaking, and I felt safe enough.

At Point Park the river is exceedingly wide, with two massive towers holding up the overhead bridge. As I paddled in the middle of the river, I spotted an empty plastic water bottle lazily floating along. I decided to clean the river a bit and retrieve the bottle. I rowed to the bottle, bent over to pick it up, and *wham*, my kayak turned over and I was swimming alone in the river. I had a life jacket and swimming trunks on. I didn't panic. I knew my overturned kayak was my salvation.

The kayak kept slowly drifting downstream. As I tried to right the wet plastic kayak, my hands kept slipping off as it steadily moved farther from me. I then saw my hat and travel bag gradually sinking toward the bottom of the river. The images of the whirlpool and the dam crept into my mind. Then the clear, coherent thought slipped through my consciousness, "Al, this might be it." I was strangely peaceful as I swam to retrieve the kayak. I knew I could not keep up the pace very long and would soon be at the mercy of the river. Both banks were quite far away.

Suddenly, and I mean suddenly, a small boat turned off its motor and pulled alongside me. Two young men, covered with tattoos and body piercings, reached out their hands, saying, "We got ya. You're safe." These angels in disguise pulled me into their boat, scooped up both my oars, and righted my kayak to pull it behind their boat. They took me to shore and waved goodbye. I thanked them profusely and, to this day, think of them as God-sent.

I was in a state of mild shock. I went back into the river in the kayak to subdue the fears of never kayaking again. Although it was strenuous, I did kayak a bit to get the feel of the river again.

Eventually I drove home. I stopped on the Pennsylvania turnpike for a bite to eat and bought the local newspaper. The headline read, "Local man drowns in the Allegheny River." I knew clearly that there, but for the grace of God, went I. My experience of powerlessness that day was total and complete.

I also knew that, during my trial and afterwards, all was well. Strange but valid.

Who Am I, Really?

INTERESTINGLY, children seem to have their personal identity down pat. They don't question who they are. They are who they are. Period. And they act out of that.

Here is a true example of the identity of a child. In my early years as a professor at Pace University, I taught a Saturday class from ten AM until two in the afternoon. One Saturday my wife and I had an agreement that she would meet me in our driveway and then take the car to go shopping. I would watch our only child, Beth, at that time aged three. It was a crisp, sunny fall afternoon. Our house sat atop a small hill, ascended by thirty-six steps on the side. At the bottom of the hill was a three-foot-high retaining wall that spanned our property, from our steps to the neighbor's property. Above the wall was a gradual grass slope rising toward the house. At the top of the slope was a plot of grass adjacent to the house that was about twelve feet wide.

Beth was sitting on her tricycle on the level plot in front of the house, high above us, as my wife and I talked in the driveway below. Beth waved and watched. Suddenly, she lost control of the tricycle and careened down the slope, screaming. She continued off the top of the wall, tricycle and all, and landed on her face with an awful thud. Her neck seemed to snap backwards upon impact. I was facing the house and saw the entire scene. From the angle of the fall, I thought Beth had broken her neck.

My wife, a nurse, was facing me and hadn't seen what had just happened. She instantly went to Beth and told me not to touch her. My wife then went directly to the house for a wet towel. When she returned, she determined that Beth's neck was not broken. We drove Beth to St. Agnes Hospital, where the attendants cared for her for a total of three hours. My wife and I were not allowed to be at Beth's bedside. The walls in the ER were white sheets separating the beds. For me, those three hours were an unspeakable agony. All too clearly we could hear Beth's screaming, until it slowly subsided.

When we were allowed to see Beth, she had stopped crying. She had a massive purple swelling on her forehead. They gave her ice cream, and she became composed, knowing that she had successfully endured a near tragedy. She looked up at me and asked a straightforward question: "Daddy, why didn't you catch me?" She didn't address her mother. She didn't talk about her pain. She wanted an answer from her Daddy.

I was dumbfounded. I knew I couldn't be defensive and say, "Sweetheart, I would have caught you if I could." No. I simply hugged her in a tender way, unlike ever before. I was so, so grateful to God that her little neck wasn't broken.

From Beth's point of view, I didn't do my job. Dads are

supposed to protect their children from all danger. I didn't do my task, and she paid the price. From my point of view, I understood that she was correct. I understood that in her little mind I was her dad, her protector. She could navigate the world as long as I was there to watch over her. Both Beth and I learned a valuable lesson that day.

Beth could be real—weak and yet strong—in her certainty of who she was and how she expected others to relate to her. For Beth, all was well even though she went through a tragic trauma. Her identity was solid.

The Real God and the Real Me

WE WILL GRAPPLE with the truth that the real God and the real me are quite mysterious. Father Hopko said, "We need to meet the real God with the real me." Perhaps the great challenge and opportunity of my life is to continue a lifelong process of knowing the real God and the real me.

The real God is totally mysterious, or to use the colloquial word, paradoxical. On the one hand, He is totally transcendent. He made, and is making, billions of stars, more numerous than we can count. He made, and is making, universes beyond counting. As Isaiah said, "as heaven is distant from earth, so is My way distant from your ways, and your thoughts from My mind" (Is 55:9). God said to Job, "Where were you when I laid the foundations of the earth?" (Job 38:4). God is totally transcendent, far beyond our wildest dreams.

Yet, on the other hand, God is totally immanent. He reduces Himself to be completely contained in the consecrated bread and wine of the Eucharist. He dwells within the deepest depths of our soul. How do transcendence and immanence coexist in God? That question is a way to begin to describe the incomprehensible mystery. That is why Jesus came, to show us in His person who almighty God is. The real God is a total mystery in Jesus.

The real me is also mysterious. On the one hand, I am nothing on my own. I am corrupt, scummy, a sinful self. We really, really don't know how corrupt we are. I heard someone say that every human is capable of committing the greatest atrocity ever perpetrated. Is that true? It is worth thinking about. On the other hand, I am a spot of light for the cosmos, a cherished child of God, supremely strong by His strength within me. St. Anthony the Great tells us about this when he says, "Expect temptation to your last breath." Although children of the Almighty, we will be children of Adam and Eve until our last breath.

Our conscious weakness is our conscious strength. We gradually grow in insight and wisdom by connecting the dots, by comprehending how our lowliness is God's opening to become our strength.

I need to continue to reflect upon me, the person within, my own unique construction by God of my energy, my personality, my character. If I do this, my insight will grow. I read a great quote somewhere that said, "If I don't go within, I go without." If I don't go within my heart, I go without wisdom, insight, and light.

We are like the airplane pilot who is continually getting her or his bearings from the flight tower. At any given moment the plane is always a bit off course, too high or too low, too far to the left or too far to the right. Yet the pilot is right on course, so to speak, and will land at the assigned airport. So, too, with us. We are always off course, yet always on course.

The real me is relational. There is no "me" without a relationship to God and to others. We relate through connectedness. Human connection is made in many ways, especially through eye contact, when the black of my eye meets the black in your eye. At that moment a fusion takes place, energy is transferred. It is the moment in the Sistine Chapel where God's finger reaches to connect with the human finger. A gap is crossed; an infinite chasm is bridged; isolation is broken. Connection is made, and the "me" becomes more "me."

The real me is an inner universe of ever-changing energies. As Bishop John said so clearly in the Foreword to this book, we are "a macrocosmos in a microcosmos." My paltry understanding is that these inner energies are primarily our relationships, more in number than we can count. These relationships include God Almighty, the saints and angels we know, and all the humans, living and dead, who were or are part of our life.

We are more inextricably intertwined with each other than we can imagine. In one sense, my brother and my sister are me, or at least make a significant impact on my identity as me. The Christian view of the interrelatedness of persons is diametrically opposed to much of the current cultural notion of rugged individualism.

It certainly is possible not to meet the real God—to have our own variations as we create God in our imagined image and likeness. If I were to recommend a book on this topic, it would be Fr. Thomas Hopko's book *The Names of Jesus*, published by Ancient Faith Publishing, which talks about the triune divinity as known through Jesus Christ, through His names. We know the real God through Christ, our friend. In John, we read, "No longer do I call you servants, for a servant does not know what his master is doing; but I have called you friends, for all things that I heard from My Father I have made known to you. You did not choose Me, but I chose you and appointed you that you should go and bear fruit, and *that* your fruit should remain" (John 15:15, 16). It baffles the human mind to think of Christ as our friend.

A Personal Testimony

I WILL NOW INCLUDE a long, edited version of an email that I received from a recent college graduate. I have changed the name. I would ask you to read this email as if it were sent to you:

Hi Dr Rossi,

We understand, through the lens of Orthodoxy, how God purposefully uses brokenness to turn our hearts of stone into hearts of flesh. This is really beautiful and profoundly true.

This is a lesson God has been teaching me in this season of my life. I was just thinking this morning how this past summer was the worst summer of my life, never felt more hurt in my life; my dad just seemed like the thorn in my flesh who would eventually crush me to the point of death. I reached a point where I thought it would be better to be dead because the pain was so unbearable.

But this past month I began to go to therapy. I am learning that these times of suffering weren't just worth it and necessary, but would give this chapter of my life much meaning and joy. This dance that happens between brokenness and wholeness seems to be part of God's strategy to help us become more like Christ, because literally the next day after I had my therapy session, I got mugged. I went from free, joyful, and liberated to scared and physically terrified all the time. But, I am slowly recovering from the trauma.

I ask the Lord please go easy on me because I am very, very weak, but nevertheless not my will but yours, because I know as He breaks he also heals, and as much as we are thirsty and hungry, as much he satisfies us and brings us to waters of rest where our cups can overflow with joy and gladness.

The beauty of all of this is that the redemption of painful times is not merely earthly; they are heavenly and eternal.

I am joyful because the Lord is present in every task, because in the stillness He nourishes my soul, because He is giving me to live for some while as a child and in that I am discovering myself and who I am in Christ.

It is the same with therapy. The Lord healed me and the gift of that wasn't just the awareness that my dad doesn't control me or that his meanness cannot change or hurt me because it is not real (he is just a child wearing a monster costume), the gift is that I can rest in the presence of my Savior anywhere; it is in trusting that Jesus has got me.

It is only through personal experience that we can understand and even yearn for God's ways. We can hanker for His healing and only through experience can it resonate with us, only through true vulnerability and experiencing the shame of nakedness and inner poverty can we appreciate to know the richness of wholeness, truth, abundance, and healing.

What a beautiful and terrifying God. He is the artist of my soul, the artist of my life both internally and externally, He gives and He takes, but I am at rest knowing He does not lead where He will not be, and He will not be where He will not heal.

Thank you for sharing, Dr Rossi, and remembering me through your podcast.

Sincerely,

Sophia

I was so deeply moved, and inspired, by her words about finding strength in Christ through weakness and vulnerability that I decided to share them with you in this little book.

CHAPTER 6

All Is Well— Consciousness

···

W HAT IS CONSCIOUSNESS? Consciousness is awareness of our external and internal reality at any given
moment. Consciousness consists of more than thought. But
thoughts, or *logismoi*, provide an easy inroad into our deeper
self, the total self, sometimes called the *nous* or the heart. Consciousness consists in an awareness of our thoughts, feelings,
and desires, our very being.

The Canoe and the Helicopter

I'M GOING TO BEGIN with the assertion that we have more
control over our thought processes than we are led to believe,
or than we sometimes give ourselves credit for. Controlling
thoughts is about freedom, freedom of one's mind, freedom *over*
our mind. I'm going to begin with a metaphor if you don't mind.
It works for me; maybe it will for you. It's about the difference

between a canoe and a helicopter—two types of transportation.

I chose a canoe for the first example because of the phrase "stream of consciousness." The phrase comes from William James, who coined it in the early 1900s, and it has caught fire in our culture over these many decades. In the first way of being, we go into our mental canoe, put it into the stream of our consciousness, and then float along and see what our consciousness *is*. That is what the human life is like for many.

The contrast might be envisioned as a helicopter. A helicopter flies over terrain, navigating and directing the motion of flight. In a sense, we are called to be aware of our thoughts, and simultaneously to know that we are not our thoughts. We are more than our thoughts. We can have thoughts and fly above them.

Well, I would simply say that for me—and, I would submit, for you—floating in a canoe along the stream of consciousness could be a total disaster. If we just get into our canoe and head downstream, we might not be aware that the stream is about to take us over Niagara Falls. Fatal. I will simply say that's not the way to go. In fact, it's not the way as taught by the Church Fathers, particularly the Desert Fathers. They continually talk about choosing our thoughts. The Fathers have many metaphors about thoughts, such as our minds being a tree full of monkeys that are jumping all about, keeping us scattered. The Desert Fathers also talk about uncontrolled thoughts leading us astray. Most human thought, if unchecked, is negative and critical.

Abba Poemen said, "The beginning of evil is heedlessness." It is clear that heedlessness is carelessness in our consciousness, our thinking.

I love our culture and love our world. I'm not unworldly except in the sense used in the Gospel. We are to be in the world but not of it. We are to be fully invested in our family, neighborhood, national and international politics, and the planet, but with the mind of Christ, a mind that is alert, joy-filled, and loving. We are not to be obsessed with the anxiety that's also inside us and inside all of us as children of Adam and Eve. The world consists in ugliness, and the world consists in beauty. Without denying the ugliness we are to keep our mind on the beauty, as best we can.

Controlling Our Thoughts

A FRIEND TOLD ME that his unreal narrative of himself can be a mixture of past experiences from others and a self he made up to get along better in his world. He said that he has come to realize the narrative he's constructed for himself is simply not true, not his identity. This friend has moderate OCD and a cognitive disorder that he takes medication to handle. He struggles much with his thoughts. He said that he's not a violent person. I know him. He is a kind and considerate person who wouldn't harm the proverbial flea. He said that he's not a vindictive person, but he does have violent thoughts that disturb him. He said that it's a relief to understand that these thoughts are only thoughts.

My friend referred to this insight as a reprieve. He said that for him, sometimes when crazy thoughts come, he says to himself—when he becomes aware of those thoughts—"Hey, these are my thoughts. They are *not* the authentic me." Then he returns to the details of the present moment. Of course, as for any human being, other unwanted thoughts come, and he handles them one way and another.

Along the same lines, an Orthodox priest, a good man and a very bright priest, sent me an email. In it he said, "I've come to the realization that my all-too-easy focus on my own unworthiness is tragically connected and interconnected to some of my own demons, that is, 'I'm not good enough and never will be.' And I easily call to mind my faults and blunders. I usually forget immediately anything good that I've done."

I'm a clinical psychologist who sees all kinds of people in all kinds of roles and all kinds of occupations. That priest's astute insight into himself, his inner journey, is a statement of the same thoughts that many people, both men and women, unearth in counseling sessions. We feel inadequate. We can remember our faults and blunders but not much else.

In psychology, thinking about thought processes is called "metaconsciousness," or "metacognition," that is, consciousness about being conscious. Similarly, today in contemporary culture there is a large, fast-growing movement called mindfulness; it's about awareness or consciousness. For our purposes, consciousness is about thought processes. The point is that we are not our thoughts; we can rise above them to be conscious of them, and then enlarge them or reframe them.

Embracing All Thoughts

SOME THOUGHTS ARE POSITIVE, as in Christ's statement, "The sheep hear My voice" (John 10:27). Christ's voice is "heard" by our thoughts and intuitions. The Book of Revelation says, "Behold, I stand at the door and knock. If anyone hears My voice and opens the door, I will come in to him and dine with him, and he with Me" (Rev. 3:20). Some of the Church Fathers interpret that door as our heart, upon which Jesus is knocking all day and all night. When we have positive thoughts, the Lord is guiding us along His way. These thoughts are obviously our friends.

I knew my positive thoughts when I nicknamed my granddaughter "Angel." For years she and I played games with her name. I would sometimes call her "Angel Precious."

She would say, "No, Poppa, my name is just Angel."

And I would say, "OK, I will call you Just Angel." And she would giggle and feign anger. We laughed. We knew that all was well.

But many thoughts are not positive. When we become aware of black thoughts, we can use them to say a quick prayer of surrender. Rejecting dark thoughts can be an inner martyrdom, because sometimes they seem overwhelming and larger than life. But all thoughts can be our friends, if we use the gloomy thoughts as an opportunity to turn to the Lord. Some of the Fathers look upon dark thoughts, *logismoi*, as gifts from God that we can use to turn and become more prayerful. St. Gregory of Sinai says that first comes the thought, then the sin; first the thought, then the virtue is enacted.

I'll talk about my own experience in a typical day. I'm over eighty years old. I experience a hole of wakefulness in the middle of most nights. The hole is sizable, about an hour or an hour and a half. I do my best to get back to sleep and try to pray. That's just the way it is. I go to bed early so that I get sufficient sleep.

In the morning, afternoon, evening, and night, my thoughts are scattered. Much of the time, when I'm aware of what I'm thinking with conscious awareness, I'm thinking worrisome thoughts. I'm thinking fearful thoughts, or thoughts of just being negative, despondent, and inadequate. That's a chunk of my thinking, and the chunk can be resentful. For example, "This person did this and this, and I am ticked off about it." Or I can have thoughts of entitlement: "At least I deserve this or that." Those thoughts come to me and to all of us. I'll call those temptations.

Father Hopko referred to temptation as the stimulus-cue, a gift from God, to turn us to prayer. We can use the temptation as a reminder to say a short prayer to give the temptation to the Lord. Temptations, which in my case seem endless, can be a prompt to say "arrow prayers" (short, directed prayers such as the Jesus prayer) throughout our day. We begin with some God-given short prayer. As Metropolitan Kallistos Ware says in *The Art of Prayer*, "All we must do is simply begin. . . . In order to swim one must throw oneself into the water."

In my own case, I've told the Lord that I'd like to use code. I have so many difficult temptations that there isn't time for me to say the Jesus Prayer every time I have an unacceptable thought, not even enough time to say, "Lord, have mercy." I say one word: "Jesus." For me, the mental word *Jesus* is code for the Jesus Prayer. Fr. Lev Gillet, in his book *On the Invocation of the Name Jesus*, says that the single word "Jesus" is the short form of the Jesus prayer. It can be code for surrendering all of myself to the Lord.

Some of my thoughts can be, "Oh, Al, you'd better start to worry about the way your students are responding, or the divisive issues in the Christian churches, or the national or international political situation." When I am aware of my thoughts, I try to say "Jesus." I may even simply nod, which I use as code for the word "Jesus." Then I try to become alert to the details of the present moment.

My mind is generally dark. Just dark. My thinking is often, "I just don't know how to prepare for this upcoming class, this upcoming lecture. I don't know what to write for the next few lines of this book." OK. That's not different from most other humans. What am I going to do about it? I can admit that my mind is mildly or seriously dark. At least I am attuned to the inside of my head and heart. Father Hopko said, "Better real confusion than false clarity." I'm aware, conscious, of my confusion. I'm just confused; I just don't know. Such thinking is much better than premature closure and false clarity, because false clarity simply doesn't work.

What is really interesting is that most of our worrisome thoughts never come to pass. We might worry about what could happen in the next hour or on the next day, or with this activity, or with children we know. When we're in the mindset of wayward ideation, we are not being very creative. Negative thoughts are not very useful; they are not very joyful, precisely because they are unwholesome.

T. S. Eliot suggests, "The end is the beginning, the terminus." The end goal is to become more aware of these thoughts and to combat them with the word "Jesus," as a new beginning. It's pretty simple. Hard, but simple. It's hard, because we want to think our own thoughts. We want to know where our "stream of consciousness" is going. This quote suggests a way to format our thinking, that is, to try to be aware of the end, the "Kingdom of God" as our grounding in the present moment.

Consciousness is a great gift that we have. Consciousness is our treasure. It is the foundation of our faith. "The Lord is my light and my savior; whom shall I fear? / The Lord is the defender of my life; whom shall I dread?" (Ps 26:1).

So the question becomes, what am I going to choose to think about at this moment and in general? Am I going to choose to dwell upon thoughts of kindness or cruelty, love or lack of love? Am I going to choose to think about generosity or scarcity? Am I going to have a joyous heart or an embittered heart?

In a psychological study on cognition, the experimenters paid volunteers to carry a cell phone. The experimenters would randomly call the person on the cell phone, morning, afternoon, or evening. The question was, "Just tell me, please, what you're thinking right now. OK, thank you. We're not going to use your name." Thus they collected megadata. All kinds of people were called at different times. The collected thoughts were real and raw. The conclusion of the experiment was that most people, most of the time, have disturbing thoughts, thoughts that are taking them down, mildly depressive thoughts, worry-thoughts, resentful thoughts, revenge thoughts, fearful thoughts. Basically negative thoughts.

That's the way the human fallen mind operates if not checked. That is where the stream of consciousness takes us. To counteract these thoughts we're to be praying unceasingly. When we try to be aware of God's presence, we try to rise above, fly above, our normal thought processes, like flying in a helicopter. Then we can become aware of God's presence. We can say, "Lord, have mercy," knowing that in the prayer God does help us with His mercy. That's what He does.

Peace that Surpasses Understanding

I WOULD LIKE TO SHARE the statement of a young woman, a recent college graduate. Recently she broke up with her boyfriend of long standing—a relationship that held great promise for her and for her future. She broke up with him for very good reasons. When she and I spoke on the phone, she was very down on herself, very self-deprecating, very glum. As we talked, I pointed out that there were two things going on: the event of the breakup, and her thoughts about the breakup. Many of her dark thoughts were about the pain she was causing the young man. He, for his part, was fueling that fire by telling her how hurt he was and how he couldn't live without her.

She and I spoke about her thoughts related to the breakup. We spoke about how she might consider her negative thoughts as temptations. These thoughts of depression and self-hatred were not appropriate for her situation. We spoke about how she might counteract these dark thoughts, how she might reframe her thinking.

The next day she sent me an email:

> It's good to know my thoughts don't have control over me, and I can use the blackness of them as a prompt to pray or call on Jesus while dismissing the thoughts. I'd also like to add that after our phone conversation yesterday I felt an incredible amount of peacefulness throughout the rest of my day. I kept saying, "Peace that surpasses understanding," and that's the only way I could explain it. That was the rest of my day.

That's what she said. We know that in the conversation whatever I said to her was from God, God through me, but it was exceedingly helpful for her to understand that she can actually counteract her wayward thoughts, and knowing that gave her great peace. In some sense she arrived at a peace that surpassed understanding.

Our Thoughts Are Our Gateway

OUR THOUGHTS are the gateway into our consciousness, our heart. Paradoxically, we could say that our heart is the gateway into our thoughts. As the Desert Fathers and Mothers insist, it is easier to begin changing our thoughts as a gateway to changing our heart. The gateway to our heart is our gateway to sanity and to sanctity. Father Hopko often said, "Sanity equals sanctity." Jesus is the sanest and the holiest person who ever lived.

CHAPTER 7

Our Thoughts
Determine Our Lives

IN A WONDERFUL BOOK, *Our Thoughts Determine Our Lives* by Elder Thaddeus of Vitovnica, we find a defining sentence: "Our lives depend on the kind of thoughts we nurture." Elder Thaddeus continues to say that if our thoughts are peaceful, calm, meek, and kind, then that is what our life is like. However, if our attention is turned to the conflicting circumstances in which we live, then we are drawn into a whirlpool of thoughts that can have neither peace nor tranquility.[1]

Our Thoughts Influence Others

ELDER THADDEUS also says that we don't understand how greatly we influence others with our *thoughts*. We can be a

---

1   Ana Smiljanic, translator, *Our Thoughts Determine Our Lives: The Life and Teachings of Elder Thaddeus of Vitovnica* (Platina, CA: St. Herman of Alaska Brotherhood, 2009), p. 8.

strong positive influence, or the opposite, depending on the kind of *thoughts and desires* we breed. He says that our thoughts transcend our words and release energy to influence others.

We can learn from children how to think productively. One fine example is the group of children who set up a card table at curbside with a couple of rocks on it, left a sign that said, "Free rocks," and then went home. What did the children hope to gain from their endeavors? That may be their little secret. We might say that the children behaved differently because they thought differently. Their innocent and childish thoughts translated into behaviors that might help adults see rocks from a different perspective.

Our Vulnerability to Suggestion

COGNITIVE PSYCHOLOGISTS, while investigating fake news, happened upon an unexpected finding. They found that when we read or hear any sentence, we are more likely to view that sentence a bit more favorably in the future. We are more likely to give that sentence slightly more veracity—any sentence, no matter how absurd or ludicrous. Suppose someone said, "If you drink eight ounces of poison, you will strengthen your immune system." You might say, "Stupid idea." But—and this is a large but—that sentence will sound a little less stupid the next time we hear it.

The implications of this finding are vast. One highly

successful businessman said, "Tell the clients a lie three times. Flatter them. Close the deal." That is, hearing the lie a third time makes it more credible. Of course, the opposite is true. When we hear or read a valid and true statement, we are likely to hear that sentence in the future with more credence. Our worldview and our faith become deeper.

So we must be extremely careful what we allow into our eyes and ears. We are careful with every word we say. Jesus said, "But I say to you that for every idle word men may speak, they will give account of it in the day of judgment" (Matt. 12:36). We also don't repeat a lie to argue with it. Repeating any sentence gives it more power. We cannot resolve not to be affected—we are children of Adam and Eve and have soft brains. And, of course, the implications are important for the way we treat children. Lord, have mercy.

Our Thoughts as Our Friends

I WILL CONTINUE TO UNPACK the idea that we have more control over our thoughts than we sometimes believe. This insight, not originally mine, is deeply profound. St. Paul tells us, "But we have the mind of Christ" (1 Cor. 2:16). Our task is to remove the debris that covers His mind within us.

For about six years I coached my son Timothy's Little League baseball team. Each year he asked me to please coach his team. I told him that I would be harder on him than on the other boys. I also told him that I would prefer to be a dad in the stands, like the other fathers, and that I would attend his every game. No matter. He wanted his dad to be his baseball coach. So I accepted.

The coaches picked the teams fairly. Each coach automatically had his son on his team. We met at Nathan's Hotdogs, had hamburgers, and pulled names out of a hat. Each year my wife and children would wait for me to come home to find out who would be on our team. We knew all the boys in the neighborhood. One year I read the list and my wife said, "Al, maybe you can trade some of these players." Other than my son, virtually all the other boys that year were young and inexperienced. Unfortunately for us, Little League coaches don't trade players.

I must admit that I was a strict coach. Little League season ended when school finished, early June. Our practices took place in March and April, a time when the weather was often inclement and no other team ventured forth. But the practice and the discipline paid off. That year our team won the division and played in the championship game. Sunday afternoon, as we gathered to play the championship game, Frankie, our catcher, said, "Coach, can I give your pregame speech?"

I wasn't aware that I had given the same speech before every game. In fact, I wasn't aware that I gave any speech to the team, ever. It was championship day and I was apprehensive. Cautiously I said, "OK, Frankie, let's see how it goes."

Frankie was a team leader, short and stocky, built like a little fire hydrant. He got down on one knee, got very quiet, looked up and down the bench as the boys sat squirming. He said, "We are here to have fun and to play good baseball. When you are in the field I want you to have your hands on your knees looking at the batter. Learn from what the batter does. No talking when you are playing in the field. Please try to learn to play baseball the whole time you are here. When your parents come to your game, you want to hit the ball when you are at bat. I want you to be silent when our team is at bat, sitting on the bench learning all you can about how to hit the ball. Watch the batter carefully to see what works and what doesn't. No one talks bad about another player on our team, or any player on the other team. We don't criticize the ump and we don't complain. Silence and learning baseball is our motto. Now, gather around as we get ready to play."

My point is that sometimes we do things that we aren't really aware we are doing. We just do what seems right, and we learn the impact of it later.

In 2 Corinthians, St. Paul tells us to "take every thought captive" (2 Cor. 10:5, RSV). If we don't, every thought might take us captive. We are often unaware of the thoughts that run through our mind. We have about four thousand distinct thoughts every day.

Combating Negative Thoughts

WHEN WE BECOME AWARE of negative thoughts, we don't combat them directly. They are larger than life and certainly larger than our strength to combat them. So we become aware of them, let them go, and surrender them to the Lord so He can combat them for us.

Our negative thoughts can be our victory in the spiritual warfare. When we counteract harmful thoughts, we receive the crown of glory.

We cannot prevent unwanted thoughts from entering our mind. We cannot be rid of evil thoughts by human thinking. St. Gregory of Sinai teaches that a beginner—and we are all beginners—cannot chase a thought away unless God does it.

Sometimes we tell ourselves the narrative we've been taught. Then we come to believe that's who we really are. The narrative we tell ourselves is not unlike reality television, a script of reality that is contrived and made up. These thoughts are merely thoughts, not the authentic us. There is a larger picture. The unreal narrative of me can be a mixture of past experiences from others and a self I've made up to get along better in my world. Gradually I come to realize that many of these thoughts are simply not true.

In my childhood my mother, whom I called Nanny, was a "pasta mamma." She was affectionate and protective, and loved us dearly. She spent much of her time cooking what we liked.

She was somewhat of a model mother, but not perfect. To make me more virtuous from her point of view, she regularly told me, "You are careless, oh, you are so careless," in response to any task I didn't perform perfectly. I grew up with one part of me accepting the narrative that I am a "careless" person. Through therapy and much effort, I have changed that thought pattern. Now I think of myself as basically a careful and caring person, to the best of my ability. For me, that change of consciousness about my self-image is huge. It can be a lifetime struggle to conclude that all is well, especially with me, even though I am a sinner.

The struggle with harmful thoughts can be a form of "white martyrdom," that is, martyrdom without the shedding of red blood. White martyrdom can be even more difficult than martyrdom by the sword, a martyrdom that seems swift and certain. White martyrdom can seem endless, unswift, and uncertain of victory or completeness.

It's not always easy to distinguish between light and dark thoughts, but we can learn. Christ's thoughts in us produce peace. Negative thoughts cause anguish, worry, depletion, and depression.

Pessimistic thoughts can enlarge during times of low moral resistance. They're often unpredictable, and they can happen suddenly; they can happen in the evening as we're going to sleep, in the middle of the night, or at times when we're sick. It's hard, then, to resist temptation. It's hard to resist negative thoughts.

Some times of low moral resistance can be remembered using the word HALT. Our resistance is low when we're Hungry, Angry or anxious, Lonely, or Tired. Depressing thoughts during these times seem more difficult to combat precisely because we have less combative strength. We might have low blood sugar; we might have a common cold; we might have some more serious sickness. But we do know the words of St. Paul: "When I am weak, then I am strong" (2 Cor. 12:10). We try to say, "Jesus," or some other short prayer. And then the name *Jesus* becomes a filter for incoming and outgoing thoughts.

Becoming Less Judgmental

THE SAME APPLIES to thoughts of judgment toward others. One implication of "all is well" is that we don't have to judge others.

We don't become less judgmental by a quick resolution to stop. Consciously or unconsciously, we all judge others. We become less judgmental by catching ourselves in the act of judging others, then surrendering the judgment to the Lord. In that sense, judging others can be an opportunity to pray, to surrender, and to be less judgmental. God can do for us what we cannot do for ourselves.

Savor the Experience

I OFTEN PULL my sixteen-month-old grandson around the house in his little red wagon. He delights in the ride. Sometimes he squeals with delight. Once, while I was eating at the dinner table with his parents, he came over with his truck, took out the wooden slats, sat in the wagon, and just looked up at me, awaiting my response. His look was expectant. His look spoke volumes. His look said, "Poppa, I know that you would never hurt me," and "I know you love me dearly," and "I trust you, Poppa, to give me a ride if you can."

Is that how God wants us to approach Him, with unconditional anticipation? Is that how God would have us format our thoughts toward Him? Is that how God wants us to have an attitude that "all is well?"

CHAPTER 8

The More Things Change, the More They Stay the Same

A BIG PART OF US resists fundamental change. We like a predetermined amount of predictability. We all have an inner control freak just waiting to emerge.

About reality, we learn one truth at a time. We learn slowly and unevenly. Father Schmemann would tell incoming seminarians at St. Vladimir's Seminary, "Don't try to jump from here to heaven. You might break your leg." New insights into reality are additive, and each new insight becomes enfolded into the deeper part of us as we continually evolve and grow. It is axiomatic that if nothing changes, nothing changes. That state of affairs becomes stale and boring.

Thoughts of Children and Parents

I HAD AN UNEXPECTED opportunity when I was asked to teach a short lesson to a class of five-year-olds. My little class

94

occurred during a slice of time in the afternoon at a parish retreat for adults. I decided to teach the children one truth: "The Lord is my Shepherd, I shall not want." I told them that this was what I wanted them to learn. I asked them to repeat the sentence. They did. I asked them to say it as slowly as they could. They did. I asked them to say it as quickly as they could. They did.

Then I had the eldest child become the shepherd, holding a long pole. I asked all the other children to get down on their hands and knees to become sheep. Excitedly they did, moving about with gusto and much baaing. They got up, repeated the sentence, and the class ended. That was Saturday. On Sunday a number of the children came up to me to say, "The Lord is my Shepherd, I shall not want." I received an email from a mother to say that on Monday at dinner her child asked to say the prayer before meals and said, "The Lord is my Shepherd, I shall not want."

Children can teach us to learn one truth at a time. "The Lord is my Shepherd, I shall not want," was the full extent of what the children could grasp. I was content and they were elated. We learn one truth at a time, additively, according to our developmental level.

I didn't tell the children what I had told their parents about sheep earlier in the day. I told the parents of the children a more advanced anecdote about shepherds, an anecdote that most children could not fully understand. I told the parents

that occasionally a lamb would stray from the flock. The grazing land for sheep is filled with predators, including lions, poi-
sonous snakes, and vultures that descend a hundred kilometers
an hour, straight down, to pick up a baby camel to take to their
nest to eat. The grazing land is not a safe place for a straying
lamb.

When a lamb strays, the shepherd puts the other sheep in
a cave, builds a fire in front to keep them safe, and goes to find
the lamb. Sometimes he finds the lamb, sometimes not. If and
when he does find the lamb, he puts it on his shoulders to carry
it to the flock. But the shepherd has a big problem. The little
lamb has learned to stray. Not a good lesson for a lamb in the
wilderness. What does the shepherd do? He can't talk sense
into the lamb. He can't continually watch the lamb as the flock
moves to new grazing land.

The shepherd has to take drastic action. He breaks the front
leg of the little lamb, then applies a cast on the broken leg. The
lamb can't walk. The shepherd carries the lamb on his shoulders for six weeks. The lamb learns that it has a good life if it
doesn't stray. The lamb gets food, water, and the companionship
of other lambs, as well as warmth from the shepherd. When
the shepherd takes the cast off, the lamb never strays again. In
point of fact, the shepherd saved the life of the lamb by break-
ing its leg. So too with us. Although we are not sheep, the Lord
does sometimes allow painful situations to help us grow.

The parents were able to comprehend that truth about

sheep and apply it to their lives. So the more things change, the more they stay the same. The parents heard the same sentence when they were children. Now the parents heard the sentence with enlightened nuance. "The Lord is my Shepherd, I shall not want." The sentence didn't change. The meaning of the sentence did.

Nothing stays the same. Change brings us up against our impermanence. Change remains evergreen. We can become curious about the change that is happening right in front of us, the raw data coming through our senses. We can explore our lives with vigor, being aware that we will never have this moment again. That's the kaleidoscope of the contents of the present moment. If things don't change, things don't change, and that can be a disaster.

Abba Poemen alerted us when he said, "We are not condemned because of our thoughts that enter us, but because we use our thoughts badly; our thoughts can cause us either to suffer shipwreck or to be crowned."

Authentic Sameness Requires Calmness

ACQUIRING CALMNESS IS A GRADUAL, slow process. Calmness will probably only become "solid state," or unremitting habit, one breath after our last living breath in this body. At least for myself, I expect that will be the case.

Am I a completely calm man in his eighties? Heavens, no.

But I am calmer than before. Once, shortly after my wife died, my daughter Beth, aged twenty, and I were visiting my wife's widowed mother, Baba. Somehow, Beth and I got into a dispute in Baba's kitchen. I could see Baba backing away from the scene as the differences escalated between Beth and myself. We began to raise our voices at one another. Unexpectedly Beth stopped, looked at me, and simply said, "Dad, who is the adult here?"

End of story. I was stopped in my tracks by my own lack of calmness. My passions got out of control. We learn slowly to be patient with ourselves as we keep our eye on the marker, allowing Christ to bring more calm into our souls in each and every situation. Life is one long learning curve.

Life Is Fragile

WE KNOW THAT our lives, our institutions, and our governments are a house of cards, to be blown away with any strong wind, scandal, or upheaval. We try to pretend differently, but the truth is found in Hebrews: "For here we have no lasting city, but we seek the city which is to come" (Heb. 13:14, RSV).

A stark example comes to mind. A friend of mine, a fellow professor, was riding his exercise bicycle in his living room, talking with a man who was sitting on the couch. One minute my friend was exercising; the next minute he was on the rug, dead. He had a fatal heart attack in the middle of an afternoon.

That true story remains riveted in my memory. We all know of similar incidents, yet we forget all too easily.

The Rafting Trip

BEFORE MY WIFE DIED, Beth, Tim, and I had to live separate lives while I took care of their mother. I would teach, come home to prepare hamburgers and fries for Beth and Tim, and then go to the hospital to visit my wife until eight PM. I offered to come home to eat with the children, but they said, "No, Dad, please go eat with Mum." After my wife died, I realized that our little family was fractured. I was bereft, worried, and anxious. The three of us were separate and grieving. We needed a common experience to bond us together again.

I prayed, and I decided that the children and I needed an eight-day whitewater rafting trip in the Grand Canyon, down the Colorado River. Father John Erickson, then the dean of St. Vladimir's Seminary, had taken his wife and two boys on such a trip, and they all loved the experience.

When I suggested the trip, both children vehemently opposed the idea. "No," they said, "everybody will be a granola bar just like you. We won't have anybody to hang out with."

I asked Father John to have us over to show us slides of the trip. Again, my children objected. "No, it will be boring."

I said, "Please, he's my boss."

They seemed to understand. After some cajoling, Beth, Tim,

and I went to the Ericksons' for slides, milk, and cookies. Father John showed the slides on the living room wall. We lay on the floor and looked up. The slides were captivating. After we left, both children jumped on my back and said, "Dad, we must go. Please get us tickets." I played hardball and said I wasn't sure, because it was April, and the trip would be in August. Bottom line, we went.

We met the group halfway on their journey. We had to climb down the 9,000-foot path to the river below. The group consisted of twenty-five people who traveled in four rafts. The next eight days were a wondrous adventure. The Colorado River is like cold chocolate milk, wide and calm except in the rapids. There were many rapids to navigate. The guides allowed us to steer the raft as we went through the smaller ones. Some rapids were thirty feet high, wild and dangerous. We weren't allowed to navigate the large rapids.

At night we slept on blue mats with no tents. We looked up at the 9,000-foot ravine, saw the stars clearly, and slept like babes. In the morning we could see scorpion tracks nearby. The guides had forewarned us that the local scorpions were not dangerous.

In the evening Beth would hang out with the guides while Timothy and I played catch with his Nerf football. I stood on the shore, and Timothy would run from my side into the river. I threw the ball with just enough distance that he had to dive to catch it. We only played for an hour or so, but the game seemed to transcend time.

I could write an entire book on the details of the trip. At the end of the eight days the children and I were a unit again, strengthened in our resolve to grow as a loving, healthy family. We also knew that the trip was a gift from their mum, and that she continued to mother them from heaven.

That trip, a trip of a lifetime, was decades ago. Since then the children and I have gone to great lengths to share time and love together. My wife, their mother, lives with more vigor than ever and has a central place at our table, in our lives. My consciousness, and my children's consciousness, changed after that trip. We could say with much more conviction, "All is well." Their mum is more of a mother from heaven than she could have been as an earthbound mother.

My Life of Change and Unchange

I SUPPOSE I COULD SAY that as I get older, I welcome most changes. And I would say that most changes that I am able to make actually lead me toward a more simplified life. I can now throw away some mementos that had much more meaning in the past than they do today. Like many, in the past I was inclined to say, "When in doubt, hold onto it." Now, much of the time, I can try to say, "When in doubt, throw it out." Of course, I am in my eighties so I am closer to the other side than are most of you reading this book.

CHAPTER 9

It Is What It Is

H ONEYMOONS ARE different for different couples. One couple I know returned from their honeymoon with renewed energy to live a lifetime together. Another couple had a different experience. After the honeymoon the wife said to me, "Is that all there is?" Both couples remain married.

God is only found in reality. Reality is different for each person. We psychologists are fond of saying, "Perception is reality," that is, the way we see things is, for us, the way things are. So we can acknowledge, accept, and affirm reality, or we can try to live in an alternate reality, one we make with our imagination. I am sometimes surprised by the way some people try to force reality into their own terms. Needless to say, this doesn't work too well.

Praying Our Experiences

WHEN I WAS a Roman Catholic monk, I had a superior who was extraordinarily bright and good, Brother Joe Schmidt,

FSC. I admired him. Now, fifty years later, I have discovered that he has written a few books. He wrote three books on a favorite saint of mine and of Father Thomas Hopko's, St. Therese of Lisieux. He also wrote a book entitled *Praying Our Experiences*. I was able to have lunch with Brother Joe recently, and he was simply a delight to be with. One of his principal insights is that all our experiences can be our prayer. We don't have to compartmentalize our lives into the secular and the sacred. All life is sacred.

I must admit that I have preconscious categories in my mind by which I classify activities as *not good, good, better,* and *best.* For example, going to Divine Liturgy is in the *best* category. Doing laundry is in the *not good* category, necessary but detracting from a better use of my time. Yet I know that Mary the Theotokos lived on this earth and probably did laundry. Yes, it is possible to say "all is well" with peace and calm, even when we imagine ourselves in any set of circumstances. Another paradox.

I was talking with a woman who is a physician who was unexpectedly fired from her job in a hospital. She was angry and crying. Yet with difficulty she could utter, "All is well." For me, she provided a fine example of the intensity of the spiritual warfare. We pray our experiences by trying to live as authentically as we can, sometimes with explicit prayer and sometimes not.

We perform all our behaviors from mixed motives. Virtually all our "good" deeds have an admixture of altruism and self-centeredness. We are aware that we are likely to receive some benefit or acknowledgment from our good works. We can't avoid a tinge of selfishness. But in praying our experiences we can become aware that the power going out from us to effect good for others is a power beyond us. The power to do good deeds is a power that originates well beyond us. We begin to appreciate that our patience, gentleness, and love come from the Holy Spirit moving within us. As we become aware of the ambiguity of our motives, we can grow in the reality of God working through us.[2]

I often have dreams about being in a school. The dreams differ but have the same plot. I am busily running up and down stairs trying to find the right classroom. I realize that I am not prepared to teach the class and that I can't find the right room. The school scene differs on different nights, but the feeling of total inadequacy remains the same. I feel like a fish that has bitten the bait that covered a hook. I have fins, not arms. I can't loosen the hook in my mouth.

My dream last night was a rerun of a recurring dream I had as a youth. Especially in my adolescence, I often dreamt that I was running, exhausted and out of breath. I was desperate to arrive at an apothecary to get medicine to save my mother's life. The running is the entire dream. There is no sequence. The dream doesn't have a beginning or ending. The dream is a

2   Joseph F. Schmidt, *Praying Our Experiences* (Frederick, MD: The Word Among Us Press, 2008), p. 101.

moving picture of running and getting nowhere.

What do the dreams mean? I don't analyze dreams. I am not sure what my dreams mean, but I do know the dreams are tapping into a latent sense of inadequacy deep within me. And, I must add, most men and women I know relate to dreams in a similar manner. We who are children in a fallen world all have deep pockets of inadequacy in our psyche. Even with this deep inner darkness we can say, "All is well."

Reality Liberates

I SAW A BUMPER STICKER that read, "Reality sucks." I was rather perplexed by the claim. At that moment I shrugged my shoulders and said to myself, "Whatever." But I have been thinking about that bumper sticker. Now, weeks later, I would use their language to conclude, "Unreality sucks." Please excuse the crass language, but I know you understand. Reality, real reality, is the only place where God is, the only place where life occurs. And yes, reality is absurd and harsh, joyful and precious. We Christians understand reality as the cross, and beyond the cross is light, joy, and resurrection.

What is "unreality"? I would say that unreality is the sum of the evil constructs of our imagination about life, our worries about the future, our interior homemade virtual reality. We are all good at creating unreality. We connect dots in a way that suits our fancy. We can live in our isolated bubble, our mind's igloo, and falsely conclude that we have everything right. I sometimes wonder if this isn't what the Theotokos meant in the *Magnificat* when she said, "He has shown strength with his arm, he has scattered the proud in the imagination of their hearts." Perhaps unreality exists only as a shadow, the shadowy imaginations of our hearts.

Unreality can take a myriad of forms. The lottery, for instance, is a mental construct. Many people say, "I know the odds are a zillion to one. But who knows? I think I'll buy a ticket just in case." But what is really going on? In the neighborhood where I live, when the lottery announces a multimillion-dollar jackpot, there is a line all the way around the block of people wanting to buy a lottery ticket.

When my mother was alive she annually sent me, as a birthday present, a card with a Pennsylvania lottery ticket inside. I would say to her, "Thank you, Nanny, for being so loving and thoughtful. But really, I have enough money, and if I ever won the lottery I would be worse off."

She would always have the same reply: "I know, but if you won you could give it all to charity." My mother was a loving pasta-mamma. She wanted what she thought was best for her son.

As I understand it, the winners of the lottery do not usually have a better life because of the windfall of money. Many people show up as long-lost friends or relatives, never seen before, to offer ways to help spend the money. More importantly, many people who win the megalottery declare bankruptcy within the year. They lose all they won and all they had before they bought the lottery ticket.

Yet many of us imagine the unreality that we are different from other people and winning the lottery would solve many of our life's current problems. I know myself well enough to conclude that I am a weak man who, if he won the lottery, would not be better off for owning the winning lottery ticket. My life would quickly become more complicated. I am not necessarily better than other people.

I would conclude that unreality is self-manufactured, a homemade version of the way life can be and will be. From that vantage point, unreality has nothing to do with God.

Reality as a Hazy Path

WE ARE REMINDED of St. Paul's comment, "For now we see in a mirror dimly" (1 Cor. 13:12 RSV), or as in the King James Version, "We see now through a glass darkly." For us, our reality is hazy and unclear. Reality is what it is. In unreality, we are tempted to think we know exactly what will happen in any given situation. But in reality, the path ahead is always hazy. We can never know exactly what lies around the next bend.

Recently I had a fascinating experience during my morning meditation. I was spending a few days alone in Boston. That morning I began the day with a visit to the famed Boston Public

Library. I viewed some murals by John Singer Sargent on the vaulted ceiling of the library. The murals were stunningly beautiful, murals of heaven and hell. There were other beautiful art pieces in the library, and I felt saturated by the majestic art I had just seen. Simply saturated.

So I decided to sit on the wooden bench in the corner and meditate. It was mid-morning; I had had a healthy breakfast and felt rested and inspired by the murals. I sat, breathed gently, and prayed a short repetitive prayer for twenty minutes. What was my subjective experience? Well, I felt like jumping out of my skin, jittery and restless. Why? I dunno. My usual meditation time back home is relatively calm. What can I say about the meditation experience? I dunno. All I know is that I did the best I could. My point here is that life is the "hazy path," an adventure that often defies our hopes and expectations.

As I walked down the steps to leave the library, I gazed at the life-sized marble statue of a regal, fierce lion guarding the stairwell. The lion's eyes were penetrating. His mane was full and stately. His rested posture belied his agility, his ability to move quickly at any given sound. There was no doubt that he was king of the jungle, or at least king of the library stairwell. I was reminded of Aslan, the great lion-king in the Narnia series. Only then did it occur to me that I am also a lion, Christ's lion-presence on earth. We Christians are all lions—fierce, yet calmly settled as His presence in our little world, the world of the Boston Public Library stairwell at that moment and the world of our surroundings as they unfold. We are His fiery guardians of a loving civilization that He creates.

That same morning, after I left the Boston Public Library, I had another adventure. I had parked the car on the street, put sufficient money in the meter, and, after the library experience, walked to the spot where I had parked the car. My car was not there. I was in an unfamiliar city; I had left my iPhone in the car, and I felt bewildered. No car and no phone to track it down. There is no need to go into great detail here. Basically, I found a man who helped me, got a cab, and recovered the car in the Boston police car pound.

During the cab ride, I had the thought that maybe the police had not towed my car. Rather, maybe my car had been stolen from the street by a thug. I could envision my Honda being dismantled, with the doors, headlights, and other pieces being sold as replacement parts at a junkyard. I would never see my car or my iPhone again. How would I recover the addresses on my GPS? How would I find the phone numbers in the contacts on the iPhone? Perhaps I would be stranded, at least temporarily, in center-city Boston. I was aware of two conflicting reactions in my head. First, I was trying to pray, and second, I was extremely distressed. When the cab arrived at my destination, the car sat safely in the police car pound. So, after paying $96 to the clerk who told me I parked in a handicapped zone that I hadn't noticed, and after a $35 cab fare, I left downtown Boston.

Somehow, during our out-of-routine experiences we need

to try to pray and to see God's hand in the present moment. How did I do that morning in Boston? I dunno. All I can say is, "Lord, have mercy." And He does. We can't measure our success ratio. All we can do is move on, in trust and with as much vigor as we can muster. We are all fallen children doing the best we can.

But I must admit that I have never been so grateful to put the key into the ignition of my car. I have never been so aware of the ease of making a call on my iPhone. And I have new questions to answer. How do I back up the phone numbers on my iPhone? How do I save the addresses on my GPS? How do I manage to look twice and not overlook the sign for handicapped parking on the telephone pole that is not otherwise visible? Life is one long apprenticeship.

That was a fascinating, unpredictable day in my life. Life is, indeed, a walk on a hazy path.

CHAPTER 10

Leisure

························

W HAT DOES LEISURE MEAN? Leisure generally refers
to the freedom provided for us with the cessation of
activities, especially burdens and duties and things that are
required by life, such as sleeping, eating, and work. There is
sometimes a chunk of time that is free from these demands,
and we find ourselves with leisure on our hands—an experience
that involves some free choice. What are we going to do with
our leisure time? The choices we make with our leisure time
can be a glimpse into our deeper value system, our root moti-
vational system. What do we really want from our life? What
gives us gasoline?

Constructive and Destructive Leisure

BASICALLY, there are two kinds of leisure, constructive and
destructive. We might conclude that there is no such thing as
neutral leisure. We're either going up or we're going down. Either
God or mammon, with every breath, with everything we do.

111

Ideally, on the constructive side, leisure is time for us to re-create, to engage in purposeful activity of one sort or another to help us gather strength. Constructive leisure can take many forms. If we have some free time, particularly on a Sunday afternoon, we might decide to take an undisturbed walk, alone or with somebody. We might be using our time to simply revive, to become more aware, more prayerful, more loving, and perhaps more productive. So leisure, at its best, is a time of rest, a time for restoration, a time to restore our souls.

Destructive leisure can be a use of our time that might be momentarily fun and satisfying but actually depletes our soul. Destructive leisure is a pleasant experience at the time, but later it produces guilt. We might think of getting drunk, indulging in internet pornography, or some other destructive use of hours of leisure time. It leaves the person less wholesome, less good.

When I was in graduate school, going for my doctorate, I was a full-time student. But I also worked half-time for a psychiatrist. I was married and had one child at the time—Beth, who was an infant. My wife was working full-time as a nurse. So my day, my week, was chock-full of tasks and duties. Almost every day I drove to Hofstra University for doctoral studies. I would leave class, drive forty minutes into Manhattan, and work for the psychiatrist. In the evening I spent time helping to care for our infant daughter and had some family time, then I would study. There was not much left over. I often got home late and would eat a quick supper. My wife had to go to bed early because she had to get up early to go to her work as an ICU nurse.

At nine-thirty on most evenings, my wife and Beth would be in bed. I then had a choice. What did I want to do with my free time? For whatever reason, I did the same thing every evening. I went to the television and turned on a broadcast of a sporting event. It didn't matter if it was hockey or soccer or football or baseball or basketball. It could be a puck or a ball, anything that involved some form of sport, college or professional. I could be content watching competitive table ping-pong. I just wanted to veg out with wine—a big bottle of wine—and some munchies. I would sit on the couch, watch TV, and drink wine. As time went along, I began to drink more than a reasonable quantity of wine. It went down smoothly, felt good, and made my life feel OK. There was no complaint by me or my stomach or my wife.

As time went along, I began to wake up in the morning with a headache, feeling a little groggy. I might attribute it to the wine, I might not, but I certainly was not going to give up my evening wine, given the size of the workload I had during the day. I began with total control over the wine. In the course of time the wine got control of me, and I could not not-drink the wine. It was as simple as that. Then I graduated with a doctorate and got a fine tenure-track job teaching at a nearby university. But I kept drinking wine at night. As life would have it, my body was able to consume more wine. So whatever resolutions I might make to quit were never really fulfilled.

After teaching a couple of years and living this way, there was an evening department party, and I went alone. My wife stayed home with our daughter. I said, "OK, I'll have a good time with my colleagues. I'll have three glasses of wine." I didn't count, but probably I had seven glasses of wine. The party ended about midnight. My department chairman escorted me to my coat. The party was at his house. The two of us stood for a moment at his front door. He said, "Al, you know, you're a really good teacher. I don't want to lose you. Please drive home carefully." Then he opened the door and added, "Have a good night."

I said, "Thanks, Richard." As soon as I heard the door slam behind me I got very angry. Richard saw that I was drunk! And I certainly did not want my department chairman to see me drunk.

That evening was a wakeup call. The thought occurred to me. "Al, you're out of control here. You're becoming an alcoholic." The point for now is that my use of leisure was destructive. Using my free time only got me drunk, and that of course brought other problems. The long and the short of it is that, in due time, I went to AA, have been in recovery ever since, and have not had an inappropriate drink for twenty-six years.

There are many different kinds of destructive leisure, but I share that story out of my own experience with a destructive habit that I slipped into and that went on for many years.

Hobbies

WE REVIVE OUR ENERGY in different ways. Sleep revives our energy. We wake up more alert, stronger. Food gives us energy. Exercise gives us energy. Father Hopko recommended that all Christians have a healthy, wholesome hobby. Time spent engaged in a hobby is energy-giving and restorative.

Some people have hobbies that involve handwork such as pottery, cooking, sewing, knitting, or gardening. I know a very productive theologian who makes bicycles his hobby. He rides his bicycle, fixes it, tinkers with additions to his bicycle. I knew another man whose hobby was toy trains. One time he took me down into his basement, a rather remote, secluded area. He had an elaborate setup of toy trains, multiple trains on multiple tracks and multiple switches that he enjoyed constructing after a day's work.

Some people spend their leisure time using their brain; they just love to sit down and do a crossword puzzle or read a book. Some people renew their energy by social interaction, going out to a coffee shop with a friend or being with grand-children. Whatever form a hobby takes, it's always construc-tively revitalizing.

Some of my leisure takes the form of hobbies. I have a lovely, long workday. I counsel students at the seminary, and I teach. Then I often have dinner with a seminary graduate. My typical day is full of fascinating people with much lively activity. I also do some creative writing and answer many phone calls. Many weekends are spent giving parish retreats or visiting my children and grandchildren.

But I also do have sizeable chunks of free time during the week. I usually choose to use my leisure with hobbies, reading, or prayer. One of my hobbies is putting together jigsaw puzzles, but of a particular kind. I use Collage.com, which specializes in creating a personalized jigsaw puzzle using a photo or image that the customer provides. The company also allows customers to choose the quantity of pieces in each puzzle.

I recently completed a puzzle made from a photo of my wife's face, taken on our wedding day. In the photo she is radiant. Her face has a soft, sweet smile. As I did the puzzle I spent time with her face, pondering our wedding day and putting her together in a new way, so to speak. The puzzle took a few weeks to complete.

There were days when I really felt that I would never get this puzzle done. All the pieces looked the same size and were a similar color. I would get frustrated. There were other days when the puzzle went swimmingly. "Oh, this piece fits into that piece and interlocks over there." Yes. Working on a jigsaw puzzle is like a microcosm of my entire life, learning patience and endurance, among other virtues.

I only allow myself a measured amount of time—fifteen or twenty minutes a day—to work on jigsaw puzzles. I'm content if I get one or two pieces together. Some days I get many pieces together, some days none. When I leave work I really look forward to going home and doing my puzzle for a while. I enjoy it. In the end, I framed the wedding day picture of my wife as a Christmas gift for my son, which gave the time spent working on it an additional loving purpose and dimension.

I have ordered more jigsaw puzzles of family photos and images of saints, including one 11 x 14-inch one that I hope to complete. But I say to myself, "If I never complete the puzzle, that's OK; I just want this to be constructive leisure." I merely want to replenish my energy. That's the point. That's really what we're interested in. We're interested in life: renewing and replenishing life, which can be defined as energy. It is energetic. It is new breath.

Currently I am constructing a puzzle that consists of four warriors killing four fierce dragons. The puzzle is complex, with much interlocking activity. The warriors seem to be helping and simultaneously obstructing each other. The dragons are being defeated with swords and harpoons in their throats. The puzzle is brilliantly colored and fascinatingly active for a still photo.

I really enjoy doing the puzzle slowly. The warrior-dragon scene is a metaphor for my own spiritual warfare, in which there are both angels and demons. My spiritual warfare, like that of most persons who seek integrity, seems constant, as I fight one passion or another. There are times when the temptations are so massive that they are palpable, almost alive and holographic. Sometimes I feel dirty and guilty after a severe temptation, feeling as if I capitulated to the evil when I haven't. I know that I didn't, but the feeling darkens the victory. The residual feeling of neurotic guilt is also a temptation, to be conquered by God's grace and my "warrior sword" of calm prayer.

The other of my two hobbies is playing online chess with my son, Timothy. One thing I learned in chess that applies to the spiritual life is how to be "wise as serpents" (Matt. 10:16). In chess I should always know what my opponent's best response would be. If I play a move that's based on my own desires (passions) without looking at the opponent's possible response, I can expect to lose many spiritual battles, and many chess games. For example, in my daily life, when I am tired and try to do my daily meditation, I can expect the enemy to provide more than the usual ugly distractions and temptations. It would be foolish for me to think this will not occur.

Timothy and I agreed that we really don't want to wham each other, but we also don't want to play in a way that just lets the other win. We play our best, hoping the other will play better. During chess I can sometimes feel my savage dragons surface. They can take many forms, particularly self-deprecation or aggression.

My own savage dragons teach me patience. We can each acknowledge and take ownership of our lightless side without giving that side any right-of-way. Our dark side comes with the package of being human, being children of Adam and Eve. We will have a dark side until our last breath. That's the way real life really is. The essential question is how I treat my dark side. Do I try to deny my failings and dark temptations? Do I give in to the darkness? Do I live with and conquer my dark side through a constant awareness of the Presence of Christ within me? Upon these questions rides the state of my joy at any given moment. In the midst, do I try to say a prayer or "all is well"?

Why do we cultivate leisure in our lives? In a word, self-care. We care for ourselves so we have something to give to others. As St. Gregory Nazianzus said, "We are not made for ourselves alone, we are made for the good of all our fellow creatures."

CHAPTER 11

Beloved Friend, Father Tom Hopko

A s this book comes to an end, I'd like to once again reflect on my friendship with Fr. Tom Hopko, whose acquaintance and teaching have been an enduring influence on my life, and, as was said at the beginning, hugely significant in the writing of this book.

Yes, Father Tom Hopko and I were dear friends, across decades. I have so, so many fond memories—endearing memories—of our friendship. We taught at St. Vladimir's Seminary together for more than twenty-five years. We went with another priest to see the movie *Field of Dreams*. We went to a couple of New York Mets baseball games with my wife when she was sick. We traveled to Louisville, Kentucky, a few times to discuss a grant from the Lilly Endowment. On a different occasion we went to Louisville to visit the Abbey of Gethsemani, a Trappist monastery, where we also visited Thomas Merton's grave. We drove to Holy Myrrhbearers Monastery in Otego, New York, to

spend a weekend. Once, at the Louisville airport, sitting on suit-
cases, he said, "I have trouble with those who say they praise God
and do not say they adore Him." He was continually pondering
God and words about God. Nothing escaped his searching mind.

Most of all I remember the dinners we shared at a Boston
restaurant called Bertucci's after we had each given talks for
a special youth program hosted by the CrossRoad Institute
at Hellenic College. At these dinners, we had no agenda and
would talk for a couple of hours over Italian food, just hanging
out. Then we would walk to a nearby ice cream shop to have
a small cup of salty-caramel ice cream—our mutual favorite
flavor. Father Tom's preferred topic of conversation in these
moments was his work with people in need. He cherished them
and his work with them.

Father Tom was a humble man who, for a year, drove to my
office weekly for therapy. Although I was his therapist, he was
my spiritual father, and I gained more from his therapy than
he did from mine. I treasure the box of cards and notes that he
sent me over the years.

I would say that Fr. Tom Hopko was the most humble and
complex man I ever knew, a man of many and varied contours
in his interior landscape. One of his friends said that sometimes
these contours could be clouded over with mild darkness. Isn't
that true for all of us? Once he got quite angry because I hadn't
recommended to him Viktor Frankl's book, *Man's Search for
Meaning*. He discovered the book himself, only to find out that

I was already familiar with it. I must admit that I was rather baffled by his anger. I was never sure what to recommend to such a fine mind as his.

He described himself as a "peasant priest," yet he could hold his own in discussions with the best theological scholars. He was extraordinarily caring and pastoral. For many years my family and I lived in Crestwood, New York, close to the campus of St. Vladimir's Seminary. During the time when my wife was gravely ill, Fr. Tom came to spend time at her bedside virtually every day.

Father Tom often said that we need to speak the truth in love. He had no tolerance for posturing or falsity. As Saint Irenaeus of Lyons tells us, "Error, indeed is never set forth in its naked deformity, lest, being thus exposed, it should at once be detected. But it is craftily decked out in an attractive dress, so as, by its outward form, to make it appear to the inexperienced more true than truth itself."

I still enjoy the story of Fr. Tom's entry into hospice, where he went to be cared for and to die. It had become clear to his wife that she could no longer provide sufficient nursing services at home, so they agreed that it was time to go to hospice. All plans were made, and finally the day came for his transition. After they arrived, Fr. Tom stayed in his wheelchair until the paperwork was completed. He was then told that he would be taken to his room upstairs. They wheeled him in his wheelchair into the elevator. The back of the wheelchair was against the back of the elevator, so he was facing out. As God would have it, a man came by, looked up at the dial above the elevator, looked in at Father Tom, and asked, "Are you going up?"

With lighthearted humor to the end, Father Tom replied, "I hope so." That was vintage Father Tom Hopko.

He had a few favorite saints he quoted often. Among them were St. Anthony, founder of monasticism, and St. Thérèse of Lisieux, the Roman Catholic copatron of France along with St. Joan of Arc. He regarded his favorite saints not only as revered persons to admire. They were friends with whom he conversed regularly. He was on friendly terms with the Other Side.

He gave us many memorable, pithy sayings such as, "Orthodoxy is paradoxy." Perhaps the single saying that I ponder most is "Every prayer changes the universe." That is, every prayer changes the color of a flower, the melody of a sound, the structure of atoms. Most of all, every prayer changes the person who prays, permanently.

I wrote of a fascinating episode in *Becoming a Healing Presence*, but I will include it here for those who didn't read that book. I was scheduled to give a morning talk at an institute at St. Vladimir's Seminary. After Matins, I tried to catch Father Tom. I wanted his blessing to hand out a quote from St. Theophan, already printed on handouts that I was holding. When I approached him, he was speaking with a woman, so I waited. When he finished, I said, "Father Tom, I have a quote I would like to share with you."

He said, "No, Al, I have a quote I want to share with you."

"No, I have to give a talk in ten minutes downstairs."

"Well, Al, then just listen to the quote I want to give you now."

Of course, I listened. He opened the book he was holding, *The Art of Prayer*, and read the exact quote I was holding in my hand. Chills went up my spine. Of all the books Father Tom has in his library, and of all the quotes in *The Art of Prayer*, he read me the quote that I then handed him on the handout. I don't want to make more of this than it is. It is what it is. But the coincidence for me was mind-blowing. And, of course, we Orthodox don't believe in coincidences.

Here is the quote from St. Theophan, which is powerful to me to this day:

> *Seek God, such is the unalterable rule of all spiritual advancement. Nothing comes without effort. The help of God is always ready and always near, but it is only given to those who seek and work, and only to those who put their own powers to the test, then cry out with all their heart: Lord, help us. So long as you hold on to even a little hope of achieving something by your own powers, the Lord does not interfere. It is as though He says, "You hope to succeed by yourself—very well, go on trying. But, however long you try, you will achieve nothing." May the Lord give you a contrite spirit, a humble and contrite heart.*

That's the point. We can achieve nothing—and certainly will not help another at all—by ourselves. In fact, when we try to help by ourselves, we often end up doing more harm than good. But when we surrender to Christ, all things are possible with Him.

One of Father Tom's children told me that one of the most memorable quotes is from his commencement address at St. Vladimir's Seminary in 2007. Father Tom said, "The first and most important thing is to know that we are boundlessly loved by God, and He blesses us to boundlessly love Him in return."

He was fond of saying, "Tell me what kind of God you don't believe in, and I probably don't believe in that God either."

He often quoted his mother saying, "Go to church, say your prayers, and remember God in all you do." And he would say, "Work on yourself, and everything will work out." Another favorite saying was, "To forgive and forget is diabolical. You can't decide to forget because you can't control your memory."

About sin he said, "You cannot sin more than God can forgive."

One of his children said, "I can't remember him ever telling a lie."

When perplexed, he would simply say, "We forge on."

I would like to end this chapter with his popular Fifty-Five Maxims, which he first shared on his podcast *Speaking the Truth in Love*, and which have now been copied and disseminated widely across the internet. I know that he originally wrote the Maxims for himself, not for you or me. The Maxims are his personal code of conduct, his little draft of guidelines that he hoped to incorporate into his everyday life. They represent his approach to the battles, the spiritual warfare that he himself fought.

Fifty-Five Maxims

IF YOU ARE TEMPTED to skip this part because you have already read these elsewhere, I would ask you to please resist the temptation. If the list seems repetitive and boring, I would say to you what I say to myself: "Live with it." There are embedded pearls of wisdom in the Maxims, hidden treasures to be found by those seeking treasure in heaven.

I have read all the Maxims a few times, and I regularly have the temptation not to reread them. But, each time I do read the Maxims I find something new and fresh for me, green and delicious. I'll comment below in italics on a few of those that have meant something particular to me lately. Which ones speak directly to you?

1. Be always with Christ and trust God in everything.
2. Pray as you can, not as you think you must.
   For me, this maxim strikes home. I meditate twice a day and still think that I, like others as I imagine them, should do the monastic hours and other prayers. That's my pride speaking.
3. Have a keepable rule of prayer done by discipline.
4. Say the Lord's Prayer several times each day.

5. Repeat a short prayer when your mind is not occupied.

6. Make some prostrations when you pray.

7. Eat good foods in moderation and fast on fasting days.

8. Practice silence, inner and outer.

9. Sit in silence 20 to 30 minutes each day.

10. Do acts of mercy in secret.

11. Go to liturgical services regularly.

12. Go to confession and Holy Communion regularly.

13. Do not engage intrusive thoughts and feelings.

14. Reveal all your thoughts and feelings to a trusted person regularly.

15. Read the scriptures regularly.

16. Read good books, a little at a time.
    For me, this means slowing down my reading in order to allow meaning to soak in.

17. Cultivate communion with the saints.

18. Be an ordinary person, one of the human race.

19. Be polite with everyone, first of all family members.

20. Maintain cleanliness and order in your home.
    I have a metabolic dislike for domestic chores, and this maxim brings me back to basics.

21. Have a healthy, wholesome hobby.
    Father Tom encouraged me in my two hobbies, online chess with my son and jigsaw puzzles.

22. Exercise regularly.

23. Live a day, even a part of a day, at a time.

24. Be totally honest, first of all with yourself.

25. Be faithful in little things.

26. Do your work, then forget it.

    This is one of my great temptations, to obsess over and analyze work already done.

27. Do the most difficult and painful things first.

    This maxim goes against my grain.

28. Face reality.

29. Be grateful.

30. Be cheerful.

31. Be simple, hidden, quiet, and small.

32. Never bring attention to yourself.

33. Listen when people talk to you.

34. Be awake and attentive, fully present where you are.

35. Think and talk about things no more than necessary.

36. Speak simply, clearly, firmly, directly.

37. Flee imagination, fantasy, analysis, figuring things out.

38. Flee carnal, sexual things at their first appearance.

    "At their first appearance," as St Anthony says, speaks volumes to me and to all the adults I know.

39. Don't complain, grumble, murmur, or whine.

    Often, with nothing to complain about, I will ravage my mind for something to worry through.

40. Don't seek or expect pity or praise.

41. Don't compare yourself with anyone.

42. Don't judge anyone for anything.

43. Don't try to convince anyone of anything.

44. Don't defend or justify yourself.

45. Be defined and bound by God, not people.

46. Accept criticism gracefully and test it carefully.

47. Give advice only when asked or when it is your duty.
    I have a tendency to rush in where angels fear to tread.

48. Do nothing for people that they can and should do for themselves.

49. Have a daily schedule of activities, avoiding whim and caprice.

50. Be merciful with yourself and others.
    From childhood, I was taught to be hard on myself. As an adult, I bought into this teaching.

51. Have no expectations, except to be fiercely tempted to your last breath.
    Expectations can drive me bananas.

52. Focus exclusively on God and light, and never on darkness, temptation, and sin.

53. Endure the trial of yourself and your faults serenely, under God's mercy.

54. When you fall, get up immediately and start over.

55. Get help when you need it, without fear or shame.

Every time I read the Maxims I am pleasantly surprised to find new nuance, a new challenge in one or another. Father Tom continues to speak to me, and perhaps to you, through the Maxims.

One oft-quoted sentence of Father Tom is, "We don't pray for anything we don't already have." And he would continue to say that we have all, and much more than, we need to live joyfully on this planet.

Father often said, "All is well." The Maxims were his way of trying to live a life that radiated, "All is well."

Epilogue

I HAVE BEEN WRITING THIS BOOK—or, better said, my wife has been writing this book through me—for two years. I have had many occasions to say, "All is well," in perplexing and frustrating situations.

No doubt, I have learned a great deal from my wife's promptings, Father Hopko's insistence that "all is well," and from my many friends in so many places.

I'll end with a favorite quote from Fyodor Dostoyevsky:

> At some ideas you stand perplexed, especially at the sight of men's sins, asking yourself whether to combat them by force or by humble love. Always decide, 'I will combat it by humble love.' If you make up your mind about that, once and for all, you may be able to conquer the whole world. Loving humility is an awesome force, the strongest of all, and there is nothing like it.
>
> —Father Zosima from *The Brothers Karamazov*

About the Author

....

D R. ALBERT S. ROSSI is a licensed clinical psychologist and Christian educator who has spoken and written widely on these topics. Dr. Rossi was a member of the SCOBA Commission on Contemporary Social and Moral Issues for six years. He is currently Director of Field Education and serves as the resident clinical psychologist at St. Vladimir's Seminary. He is the author of *Becoming a Healing Presence* (Ancient Faith Publishing, 2014) and hosts the podcast of the same name on Ancient Faith Radio.

Listen to Dr. Rossi's podcast at
http://www.ancientfaith.com/podcasts/healingpresence

Ancient Faith Publishing hopes you have enjoyed and benefited from this book. The proceeds from the sales of our books only partially cover the costs of operating our nonprofit ministry—which includes both the work of **Ancient Faith Publishing** and the work of **Ancient Faith Radio**. Your financial support makes it possible to continue this ministry both in print and online. Donations are tax-deductible and can be made at www.ancientfaith.com.

To view our other publications,
please visit our website: **store.ancientfaith.com**

Bringing you Orthodox Christian music, readings,
prayers, teaching, and podcasts 24 hours a day since 2004 at
www.ancientfaith.com